PRINTED IN BELGIUM

LISTEN TO LOVE

REFLECTIONS ON THE SEASONS OF THE YEAR

PHOTOGRAPHS, POEMS AND READINGS

Compiled by
LOUIS M. SAVARY, S.J.
with
THOMAS J. O'CONNOR
RUTH M. CULLEN
DIANE M. PLUMMER

REGINA PRESS
NEW YORK
1970

TABLE OF CONTENTS

LISTEN TO LOVE

Preface

Love has many voices. Love sends its greeting in the smile of a friend, the contented sighs of a baby, the felt whisperings of the Spirit.

Often we are slow to recognize how many voices are really love's voice.

"God is love," says John the Evangelist. "He who dwells in love is dwelling in God, and God in him."

Love speaks in many places. It leans against the neighbor's fence or comes sniffing into a kitchen filled with cooking. It walks amid the bustle of the city streets or stands on a crowded bus.

Love has many moods. Sometimes love is bold and happy or else it is anxious and hesitant. Sometimes it is riotous and demanding, or gentle and relaxed, or even sober and practical. Sometimes love just waits.

Love comes in all seasons. It rides the icy winds of winter and laughs with raindrops in the spring. It wanders through the restless heat of summer and catches leaves of autumn as they fall.

Listen to love.

Love before all seasons

The Word was with God at the beginning,
    and through him all things came to be;
no single thing was created without him.
    All that came to be was alive with his life,
and that life was the light of men.
    The light shines on in the dark,
and the darkness has never quenched it.

John 1:2-5.

The Son of God

When he established the heavens,
     I was there,
when he drew a circle on the face of the deep,
     when he made firm the skies above,
when he established the fountains of the deep,
     when he assigned to the sea its limit,
so that the waters might not transgress his command,
     when he marked out the foundations of the earth
then I was beside him, like a master workman
     and I was daily his delight,
rejoicing before him always,
     rejoicing in his inhabited world
and delighting in the sons of men.

Proverbs 8:27-31

Faith gives substance to our hopes,
    and makes us certain of realities we do not see.
By faith we perceive that the universe
    was fashioned by the word of God,
so that the visible came forth from the invisible.

Hebrews 11:1, 3 (NEB)

LISTEN
TO
LOVE
IN
WINTER

Winter is waiting and promise. Its word is often unspoken. Sometimes, too, it is sorrowful and finds itself alone.

Winter knows that love is coming--and wants it to come. It feels the pull of longing. It looks up to the sky and out to the hills and the sea. And then it begins to snow.

Love in winter is cold outside and warm inside, ice skating and fireplaces, snow and mittens.

Love in winter is Christmas. God becomes involved with us. His Word becomes flesh. He offers peace.

In winter love asks us to be open, to be honest, and to trust. Listen to love in winter.

15

Love waits and hopes

A young woman

The angel Gabriel was sent from God to a city of Galilee
    named Nazareth,
to a virgin betrothed to a man whose name was Joseph,
    of the house of David;
and the virgin's name was Mary.
    And he came to her and said,
"Hail, O favored one, the Lord is with you!"
    But she was greatly troubled at the saying,
and considered in her mind this greeting.
    And the angel said to her,
"Do not be afraid, Mary,
    for you have found favor with God.
And behold, you will conceive in your womb
    and bear a son,
and you shall call his name Jesus.
    He will be great, and will be called the Son
of the Most High
    and the Lord God will give to him
the throne of his father David,
    and he will reign over the house of Jacob
for eternity;
    and of his kingdom there will be no end."
And Mary said to the angel,
    "How can this be, since I have no husband?"
And the angel said to her,
    "The Holy Spirit will come upon you,
and the power of the Most High will overshadow you;
    therefore the child to be born of you
will be called holy, the Son of God."

Luke 1:26-35

17

Dreams

Hold fast to dreams
For if dreams die
Life is a broken-winged bird
That cannot fly.

Hold fast to dreams
For when dreams go
Life is a barren field
Frozen with snow.

Langston Hughes

For the works of the Lord are wonderful,
and his works are concealed from men.

Sirach 11:4

The hiddenness of God

I speak God's hidden wisdom, his secret purpose
    framed from the very beginning to bring us
to our full glory. The powers that rule
    the world have never known it; if they had,
they would not have crucified the Lord of glory.
    But, in the words of Scripture, "Things beyond
our seeing, things beyond our hearing,
    things beyond our imagining, all prepared by God
for those who love him; these it is that God
    has revealed to us through the Spirit."

1 Corinthians 2:7-10 (NEB)

I will open my mouth in parables;
   I will utter things kept secret
since the world was made.

Matthew 13:35 (NEB)

By the waters of Babylon
    There we sat down and wept
When we remembered Zion.

On the willows there
    We hung up our lyres
For our captors made us sing.

Our tormenters wanted us to amuse them.
    "Sing us a song of Zion," they said.
How can we sing the song of the Lord
    in a strange land?

I will not forget you, O Jerusalem.
    Let my right hand wither,
if I do not remember you.

                                          Psalm 137:1-6

Hope for a better country

All these persons of former days
    died in faith,
not having received what was promised,
    but having seen it far ahead
and greeted it from afar.
    They acknowledged that they were
no more than strangers
    or passing travellers on earth.
People who speak in this way
    make it clear that they are seeking
a homeland.
    If their hearts had been
in the country they left,
    they could desire a better country,
that is, a heavenly one.
    That is why God is not ashamed
to be called their God,
    for he has prepared a city for them.

Hebrews 11:13-16

Waiting for love

Up to the present,
    we know the whole created universe
groans in all its parts
    as if in the pangs of childbirth.
Not only so, but even we,
    to whom the Spirit is given
as firstfruits of the harvest to come,
    are groaning inwardly while we wait
for God to make us his sons
    and set our whole body free.
For we have been saved, though only in hope.
    Now to see is no longer to hope:
why should a man endure
    and wait for what he already sees?
But if we hope for something
    we do not yet see,
then, in waiting for it,
    we show our endurance.

Romans 8:22-25 (NEB)

Love knows sorrow

From God's hand

Once again the Sons of God came to attend on Yahweh, and among them was Satan. "Where have you been?"

"Round the earth," Satan answered, "roaming about."

So Yahweh asked him, "Did you notice my servant Job? There is no one like him on the earth: a sound and honest man who fears God and shuns evil. His life continues blameless as ever: in vain you provoked me to ruin him."

"Skin for skin," Satan replied. "A man will give away all he has to save his life. But stretch out your hand and lay a finger on his bone and flesh; I warrant you he will curse you to your face."

"Very well," Yahweh said to Satan, "he is in your power. But spare his life."

So Satan left the presence of Yahweh.

He struck Job down with malignant ulcers from the sole of his foot to the top of his head. Job took a piece of pot to scrape himself, and went and sat in the ashpit.

Then his wife said to him, "Do you now still persist in your blamelessness? Curse God and die."

"That is how foolish women talk," Job replied. "If we take happiness from God's hand, must we not take sorrow too?"

And in all this misfortune Job uttered no sinful word.

Job 2:1-10 (JB)

I am forgotten

To be cut off from other human beings
        and their love,
to be cut off from all sense of God
        and of his love,
to be cut off from what one believes
        to be one's real self
and to be lodged in the body of a ghost
        who has lost the power to love:
this is loneliness.

Hubert Van Zeller

I am forgotten like the unremembered dead;
        I am like a dish that is broken.
I hear the whispers of the crowd,
        that frighten me from every side,
as they consult together against me,
        plotting to take my life.
But my trust is in you, O Lord;
        I say, "You are my God."

Psalm 31:12-14

Eyes to see me

yeah here am i
am standing
at the crest of a tallest
hill with a trumpet
in my hand & dark
glasses
on.

bearded & bereted i proudly stand!
    but there are no eyes to see me.
i send down cool sounds!
    but there are no ears to hear me.

Carl Wendell Hines, Jr.

Ears to hear me

The joint, as Fats Waller would have said, was jumping...
And during the last set, the saxophone player
took off on a terrific solo.

He was a kid from some insane place like Jersey City
or Syracuse, but somewhere along the line he had disco-
vered he could say it with a saxophone.

He stood there, wide-legged, humping the air, filling
his barrel chest, shivering in the rags of his
twenty-odd years, and screaming through the horn,

"Do you love me?" "Do you love me?" "Do you love me?"
And again--"Do you love me?" "Do you love me?"
"Do you love me?"

The same phrase unbearably, endlessly, and variously
repeated with all the force the kid had ....
The question was terrible and real.

The boy was blowing with his lungs and guts
out of his short past; and somewhere in the past,
in gutters or gang fights ... in the precinct basement,
he had received a blow from which he would never
recover, and this no one wanted to believe.

Do you love me? Do you love me? Do you love me?

The men on the stand stayed with him, cool and at a
little distance, adding and questioning ... But each man
knew that the boy was blowing for every one of them ...

James Baldwin

31

When passion dies

He grows colder and colder every day,
    while I go on loving him more and more.
His coldness will soon become unbearable.
    He is too candid to deceive me ...
I am afraid to show him how sad I am;
    such silly melancholy always annoys husbands.
I sometimes try to console myself
    with the thought that it will pass
and that everything will yet be right,
    but now I feel that it will not pass
and things will only go from bad to worse.
    Father writes to me:
"Your husband loves you passionately."
    Yes, he did love me *passionately,*
but passion dies, and no one except myself
    can understand that he was attracted to me
without loving me ...
    Now I only want to sit here all day long
doing nothing and thinking
    of all kinds of sad things ...
What good am I in this world?

                                    Countess Tolstoy

I know that people get used to sadness
        and also I will get used to it,
but I am afraid to get used to sadness
        because I know it is death.

Vaslav Nijinsky

The sorrowful turn to God

The deeper the sorrow, so much the more
    does a man feel himself as nothing,
as less than nothing,
    and abatement of self-esteem is a sign
that the sorrower is a seeker
    who begins to take note of God.
In a worldly sense it is said that
    he is a poor soldier who does not hope
to attain the highest rank;
    in a godly sense the reverse is true:
the less one believes in oneself,
    not as man in general
or as being a man,
    but of himself as an individual man,
not with respect to talents,
    but with respect to guilt--
so much more distinct
    will God become in him.

Sören Kierkegaard

A stronghold in times of distress
    they trust in you who cherish you.
For you forsake not those who seek you, O Lord;
    for the needy shall not always be forgotten
Nor shall the hope of the afflicted forever perish.

Psalm 9:10-11, 19

34

Love is awake

Shower, O heavens, from above,
    and let the skies rain down righteousness;
let the earth open,
    that salvation may sprout forth,
and let it cause righteousness to spring up also;
    I the Lord have created it.

Isaiah 45:8

The kingdom of heaven is at hand.

Prepare you the way of the Lord,
    make straight in the desert
a highway for our God.

Isaiah 40:3

Watch, for you know not
    when the master of the house comes,
at evening, or at midnight,
    or at the cockcrowing,
or in the morning: for fear that
    coming suddenly
he finds you sleeping.

Mark 13:35-36

Humanity sleeps

In the strength of his truth and in the power
    of divine life, God does not ask of a person
anything that is false or beyond his power.
    Rather, God invites what is most human
in every person to become aware of itself.
    Many persons, taught to be satisfied
with narrow and confining joys, seem to be
    locked within little rooms of love.
"Humanity has been sleeping--and still sleeps."
    Deep within mankind, still asleep,
lies an immense power and truth, which will awake
    only when persons have learned to break out
of attitudes that are narrow and self-centered.
    When individuals come to recognize
the reality called "mankind," human life will present
    a new horizon of possibilities. And persons
will learn to feel at home with the far-reaching
    realities of the universe.

Louis M. Savary

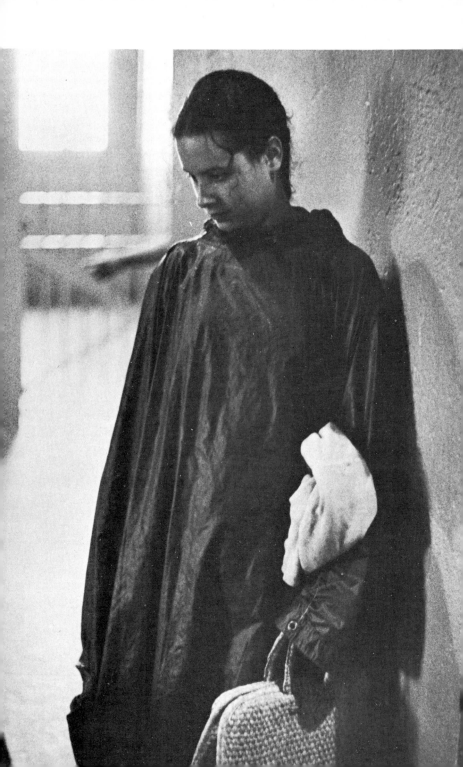

An unsettled people

We are unsettled to the very roots of our being.
    There isn't a human relation,
whether of parent and child,
    husband and wife, worker and employer,
that doesn't move in a strange situation.
    We are not used to a complicated civilization,
we don't know how to behave
    when personal contact and eternal authority
have disappeared.
    There are no precedents to guide us,
no wisdom that wasn't made for a simpler age.
    We have changed our environment more quickly
than we know how to change ourselves.

                            Walter Lippmann

Do not despise your situation:
    in it you must act, suffer, and conquer.
From every point on earth
    we are equally near to heaven
and to the infinite.

                        Henri Frédéric Amiel

Now is the time

Behold, now is the acceptable time;
    Behold, now is the day of salvation.

                          2 Corinthians 6:2

Speaking of God must engage people
    at particular points, not just "in general."
It must be a word about their own lives,
    their children, their jobs, their hopes
        or disappointments
to the bewildering crises within which
    our personal troubles arise;
a word which builds peace in the nuclear world,
    which hastens the day of freedom
in a society stifled by segregation.
    If the word is not a word which arises
from a concrete involvement of the speaker
    in these realities,
then it is not a word of God at all
    but empty twaddle.
Talk of God occurs only when we are away
    from the ghetto and out of costume;
when we are participants in that political action
    by which He restores men to each other.

                          Harvey Cox

Love is Christmas

The brightness of your glory
    made itself manifest
to the eyes of our mind
    by the mystery of the Word made flesh.
And we are drawn to the love of things unseen
    through him whom we acknowledge as God,
now seen by men.

Song of Christmas

A great light

The people who walked in darkness
    have seen a great light;
those who dwelt in a land of deep darkness,
    on them has light shined.
For to us a child is born,
    to us a son is given;
and the government will be upon his shoulder,
    and his name will be called
"Wonderful, Counselor, Mighty God,
    Everlasting Father, Prince of Peace."
Of the increase of his government
    and of peace
there will be no end,
    upon the throne of David,
and over his kingdom, to establish it,
    and to uphold it with justice
and with righteousness
    from this time forth and for evermore.

Isaiah 9:2-7

He brings peace

Blessed be the Lord God of Israel,
    for he has visited and redeemed his people,
and has raised up a horn of salvation for us
    in the house of his servant David,
as he spoke by the mouth of his holy prophets
    from of old,
that we should be saved from our enemies,
    and from the hand of all who hate us.

Luke 1:68-71

He shall judge between the nations,
    and shall decide for many peoples;
and they shall beat their swords into plowshares
    and their spears into pruning hooks;
nation shall not lift up sword against nation,
    neither shall they learn war anymore.

Isaiah 2:4

Tidings of great joy

Behold my servant,
whom I uphold, my chosen,
in whom my soul delights;
I have put my Spirit upon him,
he will bring forth justice to the nations.
He will not cry or lift up his voice,
or make it heard in the street;
a bruised reed he will not break,
and a dimly burning wick
he will not quench;
he will faithfully bring forth justice.
He will not fail or be discouraged
till he has established justice
in the earth;
and the coastlands wait for his law.

Isaiah 42:1-4

A look of hope

Let us make our approach in sincerity of heart
    and full assurance of faith,
our guilty hearts sprinkled clean,
    our bodies washed with pure water.
Let us be firm and unswerving in the confession
    of our hope, for the giver of the promise
may be trusted.

Hebrews 10:22-23 (NEB)

He comes to save

God our Savior
    desires all men to be saved.

1 Timothy 2:3-4

The question, then, is whether God *can* eventually
    do for the free creatures whom He created
what He *wants* to do for them.
    He is not ... trying to force
or entice His creatures against the grain
    of their nature,
but to render them free to follow
    their own deepest desire,
which can lead them only to Himself.
    For He has made them for Himself,
and their hearts are restless
    until they find their rest in Him.
He is not seeking to subjugate them
    but to liberate them,
in order that they may find in Him
    their own deepest fulfillment
and happiness.
    It remains theoretically possible
that He will fail;
    but He will never cease to try,
and we may (as it seems to me)
    have a full practical certainty
that sooner or later He will succeed.

John Hick

Love is confident

For all things are yours,
the world or life or death
or the present or the future,
all are yours.

1 Corinthians 3:21-22

Learning to trust

The air in which we live
    is so infected with mistrust
that it is almost bringing us to ruin.
    But wherever we broke through
the layer of mistrust,
    we found there the experience
of a trust that we had previously
    not even dreamed of.
We have learned to put our lives
    into the hands of those we trust.
Against all the ambiguity
    in which our acts and lives have had to stand
we have learned to trust unreservedly.
    We know now that we can really live
and work only in such confidence,
    which always remains a risk,
but a risk that is gladly assumed.
    Trust will always remain for us
one of the greatest, rarest, and happiest gifts
    of human life in community,
and it can arise only against the dark background
    of a necessary mistrust.

Dietrich Bonhoeffer

Through the darkness

A worm is perfectly helpless.
  It has no strength to fight
or protect itself from danger.
  Whether food for birds
or to be trampled underfoot by man,
  it resigns itself to sacrifice;
but a worm is always busy.
  Hidden away out of sight,
it gets little credit for what it does,
  yet it is the greatest blessing
to plant life in the world.
  It lives entirely for others.
A worm is of the earth earthy
  but it plows its way through the darkness,
it feeds and thrives and grows fat
  on the very earth that brings
such trials and headaches to others.

  I beg of you, Christians,
learn the lesson of the worm,
  and humble yourself before God.

Billy Graham

Without fear

So, then, the gist of the Gospel is this:
    No man is so high or may rise so high
that he need not fear becoming the lowliest.
    Conversely, no one has fallen, or may fall,
so deeply as to preclude all hope of becoming the highest.
    By saying: "The first shall be last"
Christ takes all presumption away from you and forbids you
    to exalt yourself above any prostitute,
even though you were Abraham, David, Peter or Paul.
    But by saying: "The last shall be first" He guards you
against all despair and forbids you to cast yourself
    under the feet of any saint, even though
you were Pilate, Herod, Sodom and Gomorrah.

Martin Luther

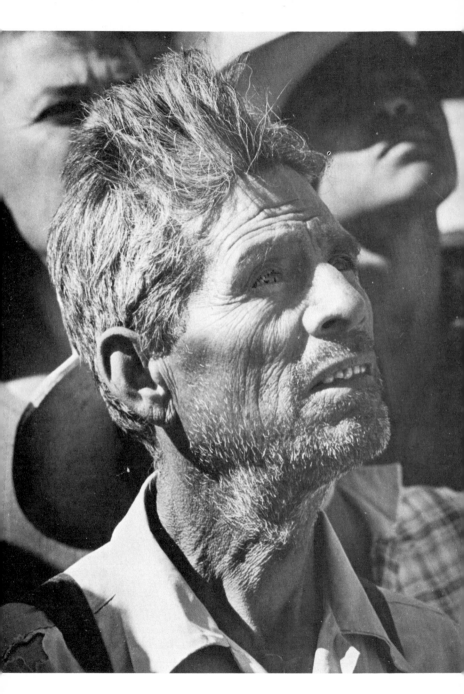

An open world

Ours is an open world.
    We are open not just to the whole world,
but to the whole universe.
    We are on the brink of heaven knows what discoveries
out beyond our planet.
    If man is around a few more hundred thousand years,
there is no telling what he may do.
    The idea of man mastering his universe
in a very fundamental way
    is not something which we hold is impossible.
In the last fifty years man has left
    his impress on the material world
in a most astonishing way.
    As Christians we should not look
at this development as a danger;
    it can be a marvelous thing.
The Book of Genesis tells us:
    "God put man in the garden,"
that is to say in the world,
    "to take care of it."
He made that world for man
    and he gave it to man to dominate
and make his own, not to exploit, but to transform.

Bernard Cooke

Love is involved with persons

God is a person

What man can know by his own power
        according to the measure of his natural powers,
his understanding, his feeling,
        will be at most something like a supreme being,
an absolute nature, the idea of an utterly free power,
        of a being towering over everything.
This absolute and supreme being,
        the ultimate and most profound,
this thing in itself,
        has nothing to do with God.
It is part of the intuitions and marginal possibilities
        of man's thinking, man's contrivance.
Man is able to think this being;
        but he has not thereby thought God.
God is thought and known
        when in his own freedom God makes himself
        apprehensible.
Heaven is the creation inconceivable to man,
        earth the creation conceivable to him.
He himself is the creature on the boundary
        between heaven and earth.
The covenant between God and man
        is the meaning and the glory,
the ground and the goal of heaven and earth
        and the whole creation.

                                        Karl Barth

What is man that you are mindful of him,
 and the son of man that you care for him?
Yet you have made him little less than God,
 and crown him with glory and honor.
You have given him dominion over the works of your
 hands;
 you have put all things under his feet.

Psalm 8:4-6

To be human

Man was put on this earth,
      as scripture tells us,
not to leave things
      the way they were--
God created Adam
      and he put him
in the garden
      to take care of it--
man is supposed to transform
      his world
so that it bears
      a mark of his own intelligence
and his own art
      and his own concern,
because only if that is there
      can there be a Christian dimension
to all this.
      If the world is going to be Christianized
it automatically means to be humanized.

                              Bernard Cooke

The hidden promise

Long ago God spoke in incomplete
        and varied ways to our fathers
through the prophets.
        In these, the last days,
he has spoken to us through his son,
        whom he has made heir of all things.

Hebrews 1:1-2

The glory of human nature,
        the form of the second redeemed Adam
that is at present so completely hidden
        even from the faith of His own,
is real only in *His* person
        and is to be revealed in us
only through an act of His person.

Karl Barth

Involved with Christ

Christianity demands ... involvement with Christ--
　　　and this is why we are reluctant to accept it.
Without involvement, however, without this willingness
　　　to become involved with Christ as a person,
all the rest is so much play-acting.
　　　Christianity then becomes merely a matter
of keeping busy.

For real Christian involvement
　　　there must be involvement with a person,
which means being caught up in my consciousness,
　　　in my awareness, in my affective life
with this person.

　　　　　　　　　　　　　Bernard Cooke

　　　　The language of faith,
　　　　　　whether that of the first apostles
　　　　or of a modern believer,
　　　　　　contains an exclusive element:
　　　　it claims the universal significance
　　　　　　of a particular, historical individual,
　　　　Jesus of Nazareth.

　　　　　　　　　　　　　Paul Van Buren

Finding the center of things

We all of us tend at every moment
    to put ourselves in the place of God
by setting ourselves in the center
    of the universe.
The new-born infant comes into the world
    as the center of his own universe,
and all his education will consist
    in learning that he is not the center
of things. Yet every time
    we mention Original Sin
we ought also to mention Original Righteousness:
    this is the other side of the paradox.
The vestiges of the divine image remain in us;
    we know that we are self-centered
and we know that self-centeredness is wrong.
    No man-made technique of psychology or pedagogy
can completely adjust us to society;
    our deepest need is for community,
for reconciliation, for right relationships
    with our fellow men and with God.
We need a salvation
    which no human technique can bring.

Alan Richardson

Everything that was written in times past
    was written for our instruction,
that through the patience and encouragement
    afforded by the scriptures we might have hope.

Romans 15:4

LISTEN
TO
LOVE
IN
SPRING

In coming from winter to spring, love suffers. But soon its suffering is turned into blossoms and bursting, grass-green joy, warm air and rainbows. It is young and free and above all alive.

Springtime is Easter when love rises from the earth, never again to be broken or destroyed.

Love in spring is buttoned and belted, ready and waiting to meet life. It is eager to try new things.

If Easter love is hurt, it forgives. If love in spring does any harm, it is quick to set things right again.

Spring love is irresistible and radiant.

Listen to love in spring as it grows.

Love suffers

Man has places in his heart
    which do not yet exist,
and into them he enters suffering
    in order that they may have existence.

Leon Bloy

72

Heavy burdens

Then said Jesus to the crowds and to his disciples,
    "The scribes and the Pharisees
sit on Moses' seat . . . for they preach,
    but do not practice.
They place heavy burdens, hard to bear,
    on men's shoulders;
but they themselves will not move them
    with their finger."

Matthew 23:1-4

The Party taught me how to do it . . .
The Party denied the free will of
the individual-- and at the same
time it exacted his willing self-sacrifice.
It denied his capacity to
choose between two alternatives-- and at
the same time it demanded that he should
constantly choose the right one. It
denied his power to distinguish good and
evil--and at the same time it spoke
pathetically of guilt and treachery.
The individual stood under the sign of
economic fatality, a wheel in a clockwork
which had been wound up for all eternity
and could not be stopped or influenced--
and the Party demanded that the wheel
should revolt against the clockwork and
change its course. There was somewhere
an error in the calculation; the equation
did not work out.

Arthur Koestler

The best of times, the worst of times

Go across the full length of this great country
    and what do you find? Material progress beyond
the dreams of kings. Vast soaring commercial
    palaces of glass even in the middle cities.
The bulldozer and the pneumatic drill, energy,
    noise, change, the fantastic beauty of the
Los Angeles Art Center and the slums of Watts.
    The lowest national unemployment rate in
many years and the highest Negro teenage rate of
    unemployment and crime on record.

The paradoxes are endless: We have probably never
    had so much moral concern or moral indifference
at the same time in our history. But business in
    America has never been more savagely competitive
or more conscious of its social responsibilities.
    It is filling the central cities with some
of the finest architecture of the age and the suburbs
    with some of the most vulgar monstrosities in
the long sad story of commercial construction.
    We have never had more prosperity and poverty
at the same time as we have now, never more problems
    or opportunities existing side by side.

James Reston

And he took with him Peter and James and John
   and began to be greatly distressed and troubled.
And he said to them, "My soul is very sorrowful,
   even to death; remain here, and watch."
And going a little farther, he fell on the ground
   and prayed that, if it were possible,
the hour might pass from him.

Mark 14:33-36

War

The First and Second World Wars showed
    that modern war is "total war"
and that it is whole peoples,
    rather than the military,
who suffer its cruel effects.
    Furthermore, we know that war more than ever
involves compulsory enmity, outrages
    against the human personality,
cruelty, vengefulness, and wanton distortions
    of the truth.

                                    John Foster Dulles

There are panegyrists of war who say
    that without a periodical bleeding
a race decays and loses its manhood.
    Experience is directly opposed
to this shameless assertion.
    It is war that wastes a nations's wealth,
chokes its industries, kills its flower,
    narrows its sympathies,
condemns it to be governed by adventurers,
    and leaves the puny, deformed, and unmanly
to breed the next generation.
    Internecine war, foreign and civil,
brought about the greatest set-back
    which the life of reason has ever suffered.
It is the unmutilated race,
    fresh from the struggle with nature
(in which the best survive,
    while in war it is often the best that perish),
that descends victoriously into the arena of nations.

                                    George Santayana

We don't know what to do

The delinquent is stuck with his boredom,
    stuck inside it, stuck to it,
until for two or three minutes he "lives";
    he goes on a raid around the corner
and feels the thrill of risking his skin
    or his life
as he smashes a bottle filled with gasoline
    on some other kid's head.

Standing around with nothing coming up
    is as close to dying as you can get.
No two delinquents
    are any more alike
than other people are.
    They do share one mood, however.
They are drowned in boredom.

Arthur Miller

For those who suffer

Suffering transforms, matures, and instructs.
    Suffering increases our capacities of love
and understanding.
    All suffering makes us have something
in common with any of those who suffer.
    It is a power of communion.

Undoubtedly, suffering sometimes hardens us.
    It does not necessarily bring us closer to *virtue*.
But it always brings us closer to truth.

Suffering and death are the only unavoidable obstacles
    which compel the most mediocre man
to call himself into question, to detach himself
    from his existence, and to ask himself
what would permit him to transcend it.

What neither love, nor prayer, nor poetry, nor art
    could do for most people, only death and suffering
are capable of demanding.

But maybe the day will come when love, art, and prayer
    will have enough power over us so that
we might be exempt from suffering and death.

                                        Louis Evely

War no more

Ah, sinful nation,
    a people laden with iniquity,
offspring of evildoers,
    sons who deal corruptly!
They have forsaken the Lord,
    they have despised
the Holy One of Israel,
    they are utterly estranged.

Come now, let us reason together,
    says the Lord:
though your sins are like scarlet,
    they shall be as white as snow;
though they are red like crimson,
    they shall become like wool.

He shall judge between the nations,
    and shall decide for many peoples;
and they shall beat their swords into
    plowshares,
and their spears into pruning hooks;
    nation shall not lift up sword
against nation,
    neither shall they learn war any more.
Come let us walk in the light
    of the Lord, our God.

Isaiah 1:4, 18; 2:4-5

Love is always ready

And the Pharisees and Sadducees came, and to test him they asked him to show them a sign from heaven.
He answered them, "When it is evening, you say, 'It will be fair weather; for the sky is red.' And in the morning, 'It will be stormy today; for the sky is red and threatening.' "You know how to interpret the appearance of the sky, but you cannot interpret the signs of the times. An evil and adulterous generation seeks for a sign, but no sign shall be given to it except the sign of Jonah."

Matthew 16:1-4

To accept the cross

Now the Christian, raised in a new world,
    must see the cross and asceticism
in a new way.
    It is important here that we learn
to accept a cross
    which makes us always
open and adaptable to a world
    which is in continuous change.

To accept the cross
    is to will the constant modification
of ourselves and, if necessary,
    an upheaval of the values
in the world around us,
    by allowing the clear light
of the word of God to affect us.

                                        Pierre Babin

The source of strength

Therefore take the whole armor of God,
    that you may be able to withstand
in the evil day,
    and having done all, to stand.
Stand therefore,
    having girded your loins with truth,
and having shod your feet
    with the equipment of the gospel of peace;
above all taking the shield of faith,
    with which you can quench
all the flaming darts of the evil one.

Ephesians 6:13-16

The Spirit prays in us

In the same way the Spirit comes
    to the aid of our weakness.
We do not even know how we ought to pray,
    but through our inarticulate groans
the Spirit himself is pleading for us,
    and God who searches our inmost being
knows what the Spirit means,
    because he pleads for God's own people
in God's own way.

Romans 8:26-28 (NEB)

Praying

I find myself endurable
    only when I can forget myself,
when I can get away from myself by prayer
    and find life in You.

Is my life really no more
    than a single short aspiration,
and all my prayers
    just different formulations of it
in human words?

Prayer can be real prayer,
    even when it is not filled with bliss.
Prayer can be like a slow interior bleeding,
    in which grief and sorrow
make the heart's blood of the inner man
    trickle away silently
into his own unfathomed depths.

                                    Karl Rahner

Born from spirit

Jesus said, "Unless a man has been born over again
he cannot see the kingdom of God."

"But how is it possible," said Nicodemus, "for a man
to be born when he is old? Can he enter his mother's
womb a second time and be born?"

Jesus answered, "In truth I tell you, no one can enter the
kingdom of God without being born from water and spirit.
Flesh can give birth only to flesh; it is spirit that gives
birth to spirit. You ought not to be astonished, then,
when I tell you that you must be born over again.

"The wind blows where it wills; you hear the sound of it,
but you do not know where it comes from, or where it is
going. So with everyone who is born from spirit."

Nicodemus replied, "How is this possible?"

Jesus said, "God loved the world so much that he gave
his only Son, that everyone who has faith in him may not
die but have eternal life.

"The light has come into the world, but men preferred
darkness to light because their deeds were evil. Bad
men all hate the light and avoid it, for fear their
practices should be shown up. The honest man comes to
the light so that it may be clearly seen that God is
in all he does. '

John 3:3-9, 16, 19-21 (NEB)

A new context of life

The ultimate divine responsibility for the universe
    of which we are a part,
and our personal responsibility for our own actions,
    do not clash with one another.
The sinner cannot shed any of his guilt
    upon his Maker.
We remain responsible for our sins
    and subject to God's condemnation and revulsion.
Nevertheless, our awareness
    in faith of the universal divine purpose
and activity, which is the ultimate context
    of our life, makes a vital difference.
Our sinfulness is no longer a matter
    for final despair:
God's saving purpose continually sets before us
    the possibility of repentance and a new life.
For the divine love ... is able so to reconcile us
    to reality that we may renounce
our own small self-enclosed circles of meaning
    and receive a place in the universal kingdom of God.

John Hick

Dedicated service

Therefore, my brothers, I implore you
    by God's mercy to offer your very selves
to him: a living sacrifice, dedicated and
    fit for his acceptance, the worship
offered by mind and heart.

Romans 12:1 (NEB)

Do you give service?
    Give it as in the strength
which God supplies. In all
    things so act that the glory
may be God's through Jesus Christ;
    to him belong glory and power
for ever and ever.

1 Peter 4:11 (NEB)

A new mind

But that is not how you learned Christ.
    For were you not told of him, were you
not as Christians taught the truth in Jesus?--
    that, leaving your former way of life,
you must lay aside that old human nature which,
    deluded by its lusts, is sinking towards
death. You must be made new in mind and spirit,
    and put on the new nature of God's creating,
which shows itself in the just and devout life
    called for by the truth.

Ephesians 4:21-24 (NEB)

Love forgives

And when they reached the place
   called The Skull they crucified him there.
Jesus said, "Father, forgive them. They
   do not know what they are doing."

Luke 23:33-34

The sign of forgiveness

This doctrine of the cross
        is sheer folly
to those on their way
        to ruin,
but to us who are on the way
        to salvation
it is the power of God.
        We proclaim Christ--yes,
Christ nailed to the cross.
        to those who have heard
his call,
        Jews and Greeks alike,
he is the power of God
        and the wisdom of God.

                    1 Corinthians 1:18, 22-24 (NEB)

The hurt of failure

Croft stared at the mountain.
    The inviolate elephant
brooding over the jungle
    and the paltry hills.

It was pure and remote.
    In the late afternoon sunlight
it was velvet green and rock blue
    and the brown of light earth,
made of another material
    than the fetid jungle before it.

The old torment burned in him again.
    A stream of wordless impulses
beat in his throat
    and he had again
the familiar and inexplicable tension
    the mountain always furnished him.
To climb that.

He had failed,
    and it hurt him vitally.
His frustration was loose again.
    He would never have another opportunity
to climb it.
    And yet he was wondering
if he could have succeeded.
    If he had gone alone,
the fatigue of the other men
    would not have slowed him
but he would not have had their company,
    and he realized suddenly
that he could not have gone without them.

Norman Mailer

The hurt of sin

God's gift of relationship with him
    and with one another,
with all that it promises of fulfillment,
    is denied us by our sin.
We can understand this sin as being our assertion
    that we are sufficient of ourselves,
that we do not need relationship
    with God or man.
We fear men and hurt them
    and exploit not only persons but things.

Indeed, the worst hurt any of us can experience
    is the hurt suffered at the hands
of someone we love and from whom we expect love.
    Personal hurts hurt on the inside;
the others hurt on the outside.
    Inside hurts are more injurious
than outside ones because
    we are dependent on one another;
and when we have been hurt by another person,
    there is the feeling that we have been
cut off from him, with the consequent anxiety
    that to a greater or lesser extent
we will cease *to be.*

Reuel L. Howe

The just and the unjust

"You have heard that it was said,
　　'An eye for an eye and a tooth for a tooth.'
But I say to you, Do not resist one who is evil."
　　But I say to you, Love your enemies and pray
for those who persecute you, so that you
　　may be sons of your Father who is in heaven;
for he makes his sun rise on the evil
　　and on the good, and sends rain
on the just and on the unjust."

Matthew 5:38-39, 44-45

Friends again

So if you are offering your gift at the altar,
    and there remember that your brother
has something against you, leave your gift
    there before the altar and go;
first be reconciled to your brother,
    and then come and offer your gift.

Matthew 5:23-24

Love waits in silence

But Mary kept all these things,
    pondering them in her heart.

Luke 2:19

The work of silence

Silence is the element
    in which great things fashion themselves together,
that at length they may emerge,
    full-formed and majestic,
into the daylight of life,
    which they are henceforth to rule.

Speech is of time, silence is of eternity.

It is only when life is sluggish within us
    that we speak:
only at the moment when reality lies far away,
    and we do not wish to be conscious of brethren.
And no sooner do we speak
    than something warns us
that the divine gates are closing.
    There is an instinct
of the superhuman truths within us
    which warns us that it is dangerous to be silent
with one whom we do not wish to know,
    or do not love:
for words may pass between men,
    but let silence have its instance of activity,
and it will never efface itself.

                      Maurice Maeterlinck

To Look at Any Thing

To look at any thing,
If you would know that thing,
You must look at it long:
To look at this green and say
'I have seen spring in these
Woods; will not do--you must
Be the thing you see:
You must be the dark snakes of
Stems and ferny plumes of leaves,
You must enter in
To the small silences between
The leaves,
You must take your time
And touch the very peace
They issue from.

John Moffitt

Gone forever

Halfway through shaving, it came--
    the word for a poem.
I should have scribbled it
    on the mirror with a soapy finger,
or shouted it to my wife in the kitchen,
    or muttered it to myself till it ran
in my head like a tune.

But now it's gone with the whiskers
    down the drain. Gone forever,
like the girls I never kissed,
    and the places I never visited--
the lost lives I never lived.

                              Barriss Mills

Be quiet for this day is holy.

                              Nehemiah 8:11

103

The silent struggle within

The artist descends within himself,
    and in that lonely region of stress and strife,
if he be deserving and fortunate,
    he finds the terms of his appeal.
His appeal is made to our less obvious capacities:
    to that part of our nature which,
because of the warlike conditions of existence,
    is necessarily kept out of sight.
The artist appeals to that part of our being
    which is not dependent on wisdom:
to that in us which is a gift and not an acquisition.
    He speaks to our capacity for delight and wonder,
to the sense of mystery surrounding our lives;
    to our sense of pity, and beauty, and pain;
to the latent feeling of fellowship with all creation.

Joseph Conrad

Hidden in faith

Faith is obscure because
    it is the revelation
of a *divine* person
    through a *human* testimony.
This time, the barrier
    is quite impenetrable.
A human person,
    while remaining veiled,
reveals himself through his testimony--
    his presence and action--
by signs which are homogeneous and adequate.
    But through a human testimony,
a divine person can only be
    forever plunged in darkness--
"Hidden under the veil of faith
    and as if enveloped in a cloud."

Jean Mouroux

This passing age

Scripture says, "I will destroy the wisdom
     of the wise, and bring to nothing
the cleverness of the clever."
     Where is your wise man now,
your man of learning, or your subtle debater--
     limited, all of them, to this passing age?
God has made the wisdom of this world look foolish.

1 Corinthians 1:19-20 (NEB)

And you will have confidence

Surely then you will lift your face without blemish;
    you will be secure, and will not fear.
You will forget your misery; and you will remember it
    as waters that have passed away.
And your life will be brighter than the noonday;
    its darkness will be like the morning.
And you will have confidence, because there is hope;
    and you will be protected
        and take your rest in safety.
You will lie down, and none will make you afraid;
    many will entreat your favor.

Job 11:15-19

At that moment, when the world around him
    melted away,
when he stood alone like a star
    in the heavens,
he was overwhelmed by a feeling
    of icy despair,
but he was more firmly himself than ever.
    That was the last shudder
of his awakening,
    the last pains of birth.

Hermann Hesse

Love is Easter

God not only raised our Lord from the dead,
he will also raise us by his power.

1 Corinthians 6:14

Resurrection is to life

The churches loudly assert: we preach Christ crucified! But in so doing, they preach only half of the passion, and do only half their duty. The creed says: " He was crucified, died, and was buried. ... the third day he rose again from the dead." And again "I believe in the resurrection of the body, " so that to preach Christ crucified is to preach half the truth.

It is the business of the Church to preach Christ born among men which is Christmas, Christ crucified which is Good Friday, and Christ risen which is Easter. And after Easter, till November and All Saints, and till Annunciation, the year belongs to the risen Lord : that is all the full flowering summer and the autumn of wheat and fruit. All belong to Christ risen.

But the churches insist on Christ crucified and rob us of the blossom and fruit of the year.

The *resurrection is to life,* not to death. Can I not then walk this earth in gladness being risen from sorrow? Is the flesh that was crucified become as poison to the crowds in the street, or is it a strong blossoming out of the earth's humus?

D. H. Lawrence

Welcome to spring

Sing to the Lord with thanksgiving;
make melody to our God upon the lyre!
He covers the heavens with clouds,
he prepares rain for the earth,
he makes grass grow upon the hills.

Psalm 147:7-8

A song of lovers

The voice of my beloved!
    Behold, he comes,
leaping upon the mountains,
    bounding over the hills.
My beloved is like a gazelle,
    or a young stag.
Behold, there he stands
    behind our wall,
gazing in at the windows,
    looking through the lattice.
My beloved speaks and says to me:
    "Arise, my love, my fair one,
      and come away;
for lo, the winter is past,
    the rain is over and gone.
The flowers appear on the earth,
    the time of singing has come,
and the voice of the turtledove
    is heard in our land.
The fig tree puts forth its figs,
    and the vines are in blossom;
      they give forth fragrance.
Arise, my love, my fair one,
    and come away.
O my dove, in the clefts of the rock,
    in the covert of the cliff,
let me see your face,
    let me hear your voice,
for your voice is sweet,
    and your face is comely."
My beloved is mine and I am his,
    he pastures his flock among the lilies.
Until the day breathes
    and the shadows flee,
turn, my beloved, be like a gazelle,
    or a young stag upon rugged mountains.

Song of Solomon 2:8-17

And you want to travel with Him

And Jesus was a sailor
When He walked upon the water
And He spent a long time watching
From His lonely wooden tower.

And when He knew for certain
Only drowning men could see Him
He said "All men will be sailors then
Until the sea shall free them."

But He Himself was broken
Long before the sky would open
Forsaken almost human
He sank beneath your wisdom like a stone.

And you want to travel with Him
And you want to travel blind
And you think maybe you'll trust Him
For He's touched your perfect body
   with His mind.

Leonard Cohen

114

The Lord sent forth his word to heal them
　　and to snatch them from destruction
Let them give thanks to the Lord for his kindness
　　and his wondrous deeds to the children of men.

Psalm 106:20-21

Christ our Lord

The mystery of God, and thus also of Jesus Christ,
     is that he, this one, this man, by his being one . . .
not only exists for himself but is this one for all.
     You must try to read the New Testament
from the standpoint of this 'for us.'
     For the entire existence of this man,
who stands in the center,
     is determined by the fact that it is a human existence,
achieved and accomplished not only in its own framework
     and with its own meaning in itself,
but for all others.

     In this one man God sees every man, all of us,
as through a glass . . . And we may, and should,
     understand ourselves as men seen by God
in him, in this man,
     as men made known to him in this way.
In him he has from eternity
     bound himself to each, to all.
Along the entire line it holds,
     from the creatureliness of man,
through the misery of man,
     to the glory promised to man.

Everything is decided about us in him,
  in this one man.
For us it is intended that we may serve him
  in eternal righteousness, innocence and blessedness,
even as he has risen from death,
  lives and rules in eternity.
Such is God's wise dispensation,
  this cohesion of each man and all men with this one.
And that is, seen so to speak from above,
  the basis of the lordship of Jesus Christ.

The community knows that Jesus Christ is our Lord,
  it is known in the Church.
But the truth of 'our lord' does not depend
  on our knowing or acknowledging it
or on the existence of a congregation
  where it is discerned and expressed;
it is because Jesus Christ is our Lord
  that he can be known and proclaimed as such.
But no one knows as a matter of course
  that all men have their Lord in him.
This knowledge is a matter of our election and calling,
  a matter of the community gathered together by his
  word,
a matter of the Church.

Karl Barth

The door is open

It was hidden for long ages in God
    the creator of the universe,
in order that now, through the church,
    the wisdom of God in all its
varied forms might be made known
    to the rulers and authorities.
This is in accord with his age-long purpose,
    which he achieved in Christ Jesus our Lord.

Ephesians 3:10-11 (NEB)

These are the words of the holy one,
    the true one who holds the key of David;
when he opens none may shut,
    when he shuts none may open:
I know all your ways; and look, I have set
    before you an open door, which no one can shut.

Revelation 3:7-8 (NEB)

In the name of Jesus

One day at three in the afternoon, the hour of prayer, Peter and John were on their way up to the temple. Now a man who had been a cripple from birth used to be carried there and laid every day by the gate of the temple called 'Beautiful Gate,' to beg from people as they went in.

When he saw Peter and John on their way into the temple he asked for charity.

But Peter fixed his eyes on him, as John did also, and said, 'Look at us.' Expecting a gift from them, the man was all attention.
And Peter said, 'I have no silver or gold; but what I have I give you: in the name of Jesus Christ of Nazareth, walk.'

Then he grasped him by the right hand and pulled him up; and at once his feet and ankles grew strong; he sprang up, stood on his feet, and started to walk. He entered the temple with them, leaping and praising God as he went.

Everyone saw him walking and praising God, and when they recognized him as the man who used to sit begging at Beautiful Gate, they were filled with wonder and amazement at what had happened to him.

Acts 3:1-10 (NEB)

Love is alive

Alive to God in Christ

If you believe that Christ has risen
    from the dead,
you must believe also that you yourselves
    have likewise risen with him . . .
and if you believe yourselves
    dead with Christ,
you must believe that
    you will also live with him;
and if you believe that Christ
    is dead to sin
and lives to God,
    you too must be dead to sin
and alive to God.

Origen

Nothing is so beautiful as spring

Nothing is so beautiful as spring--
      When weeds, in wheels, shoot long and lovely and lush;
      Thrush's eggs look little low heavens, and thrush
Through the echoing timber does so rinse and wring
The ear, it strikes like lightnings to hear him sing;
      The glassy peartree leaves and blooms, they brush
      The descending blue; that blue is all in a rush
With richness; the racing lambs too have fair their fling.

What is all this juice and all this joy?
      A strain of the earth's sweet being in the beginning
In Eden garden.--Have, get, before it cloy,
      Before it cloud, Christ, lord, and sour with sinning,
Innocent mind and Mayday in girl and boy,
      Most, O maid's child, thy choice and worthy the winning.

                                        Gerard Manley Hopkins

Return to life

But we believe that having died with Christ
　　we shall return to life with him:
Christ, as we know, having been raised from
　　the dead will never die again.
Death has no power over him any more.
　　When he died, he died, once for all,
to sin, so his life now is life with God;
　　and in that way, you too must consider
yourselves to be dead to sin
　　but alive for God in Christ Jesus.

Romans 6:8-11

Awake

Who was ever so wake
As this wakening day?
Not just brooklet and brake,
but the roof, too, is gay,

With its tiles that outstand
In the blue of the sky,
As alive as a land
And as full of reply.

Breathing thanks are conveyed.
All nocturnal affliction
Has vanished with night,

Whose darkness was made
--O pure contradiction!--
From legions of light.

                    Rainer Maria Rilke

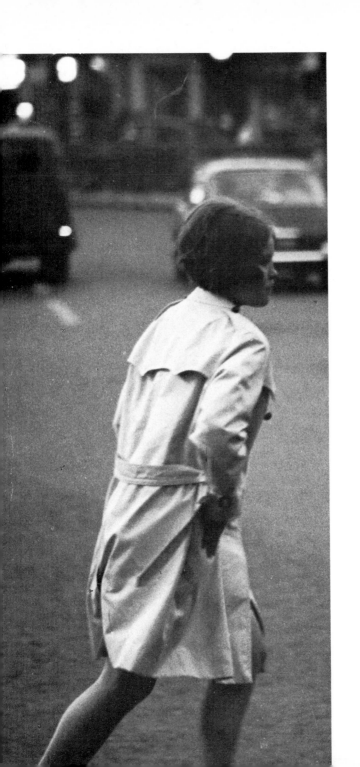

Go out in joy

For you shall go out in joy,
    and be led forth in peace;
the mountains and the hills before you
    shall break forth into singing,
and all the trees of the field
    shall clap their hands.
Instead of the thorn
    shall come up the cypress;
instead of the brier
    shall come up the myrtle;
and it shall be to the Lord for a memorial,
    for an everlasting sign
which shall not be cut off.

                              Isaiah 55:12-13

In him we move

Swift things are beautiful:
    Swallows and deer,
And lightning that falls
    Bright-veined and clear,
Rivers and meteors,
    Wind in the wheat,
The strong-withered horse,
    The runner's sure feet.

And slow things are beautiful:
    The closing of day,
The pause of the wave
    That curves downward to spray,
The ember that crumbles,
    The opening flower,
And the ox that moves on
    In the quiet of power.

Elizabeth Coatsworth

In him we live

For the love of Christ leaves us no choice,
     when once we have reached the conclusion
that one man died for all and therefore
     all mankind has died. His purpose in
dying for all was that men, while still in life,
     should cease to live for themselves,
and should live for him who for their sake
     died and was raised to life.

                                        2 Corinthians 5:14-15 (NEB)

          The God who created the world
               and everything in it, and
          who is Lord of heaven and earth,
               does not live in shrines
          made by men. He is not far
               from each of us, for in him
          we live and move, in him we exist.

                                        Acts 17:24, 27-28 (NEB)

Love is young

No limit to our hopes

No young man believes he shall ever die.
    There is a feeling of eternity in youth
which makes amends for everything. To be young
    is to be as one of the immortals.
There is no line drawn, and we see no limit
    to our hopes and wishes.
Death, old age, are words without a meaning,
    a dream, a fiction, with which we have
nothing to do. Others may have undergone, or
    may still undergo them--we "bear a charmed life,"
which laughs to scorn all such idle fancies.
    It is the simplicity, and, as it were,
abstractedness of our feelings in youth that
    (so to speak) identifies us with nature.

William Hazlitt

Only in spring

A Light exists in spring
    Not present on the year
At any other period.
    When March is scarcely here

A color stands abroad
    On solitary hills
That science cannot overtake,
    But human nature *feels*.

It waits upon the lawn,
    It shows the furthest tree
Upon the furthest slope we know;
    It almost speaks to me.

Then, as horizons step,
    Or noons report away,
Without the formula of sound,
    It passes, and we stay:

A quality of loss
    Affecting our content,
As trade has suddenly encroached
    Upon a sacrament.

Emily Dickinson

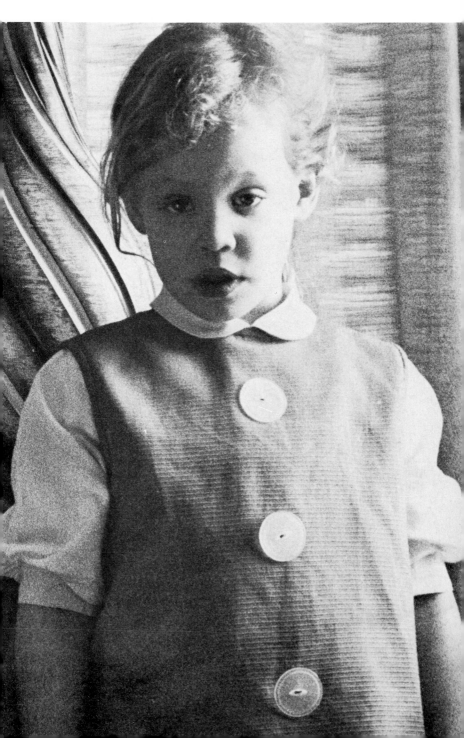

Letter from camp

Dear Sister,
    I am having a good time. I miss you very much. I promise not to fight with you any more when I come home. But you must promise not to be a pain in the neck.

                         Your big brother,

                              Phil

Like a Child

Like a child I just sat in the sunlight
and played with the minutes as they went running by.
Like a child who had never known sorrow
I didn't hurry tomorrow I just looked at the sky.
While the clouds went on endlessly passing.
All the clouds on their long voyage home
seemed to say that youth is everlasting
but a rose cannot grow alone.

Like a child I would listen in silence
to the soft sound of evening as it caught up the day,
till you were there in the gathering darkness
and we found that our green years had all gone away.
Now the clouds are going forever
here awhile then gone evermore
and a child on the far side of never
has to run when time closes the door.

Then take my hand and as children we'll go now
all alone through the thundering crowds.
Take my hand and together we'll look now
like a child for the little lost clouds.

Rod McKuen

Love is free

Freedom in Jesus Christ

The believer is free to accept himself,
    convinced that he is acceptable,
for he has been set free by Jesus of Nazareth.
    His acceptance is simply
his trust in the declaration,
    "neither do I condemn you,"
and he acknowledges this word and its speaker,
    not his own history,
as the basis of his perspective.
    He is set free and at the same time
he is set on a specific road.
    One action is a movement,
a pressing forward, a task
    in which he lives.
Considered once more as language
    expressing the Christian's perspective,
the doctrine of sanctification
    clarifies the perspective,
the doctrine of sanctification
    clarifies the nature of his freedom:
like the freedom of Jesus himself,
    it is freedom to be concerned and compassionate,
to become involved for the sake of our neighbor
    in the world about us.

                                    Paul Van Buren

Man is what he chooses to be

In death and judgment
  man's naked reality is manifest.
Death is no mere superficial change
  nor is judgment only an external reaction
to man's actions during life.
  At death and judgment the personal condition
a man has chosen for himself
  is completed and made final.
True, this final self-determination
  is achieved in dialogue with or against God,
and would be impossible without God's free creation
  and gratuitous grace. Nor can we forget
that freedom never totally determines
  any concrete life-situation.
Other determinants inevitably enter
  each individual decision.
But none of this alters
  what is to the Christian a self-evident fact:
that freedom enables man
  to determine himself irrevocably,
to be for all eternity what he himself
  has chosen to make himself.
In his freedom, man is his own burden
  and responsibility.
Freedom is creative, and its creature is man--
  in his own final disposition of himself.
Man is essentially a freedom-event.
  As established by God,
and in his very nature,
  he is unfinished. He does not live
in some ethereal and pure essence
  but freely determines
his own everlasting nature
  and bears ultimate responsibility for it.

                                        Karl Rahner

Alive and free

If you be risen with Christ,
    seek those things which are above,
where Christ sits on the right hand of God.

Colossians 3:1

Therefore, since Jesus was delivered to you
    as Christ and Lord, live your lives
in union with him. Be rooted in him;
    be built in him; be consolidated in the faith
you were taught.

Colossians 2:6-7 (NEB)

Free for a purpose

Due to my involvement in the struggle
      for the freedom of my people,
I have known very few quiet days
      in the last few years.
I have been arrested five times
      and put in Alabama jails.
My home has been bombed twice.
      A day seldom passes that my family and I
are not the recipients of threats of death.
      I have been the victim of a near-fatal stabbing.

So in a real sense I have been battered
      by the storms of persecution.
I must admit that at times I have felt
      that I could no longer bear such a heavy burden,
and have been tempted to retreat
      to a more quiet and serene life.
But every time such a temptation appeared,
      something came to strengthen my determination.
I have learned now that the Master's burden is light
      precisely when we take his yoke upon us.

                                  Martin Luther King

Inner freedom

There is not a single true work of art
        that has not in the end
added to the inner freedom of each person
        who has known and loved it.
Yes, that is the freedom I am praising
        and it is what helps me through life.
An artist may make a success
        or a failure of his work.
He may make a success
        or a failure of his life.
But if he can tell himself that,
        finally, as a result of his long effort,
he has eased or decreased
        the various forms of bondage
weighing upon men, then in a sense
        he is justified and, to some extent,
he can forgive himself.

Albert Camus

Love tries new things

A new quality

This world of ours is a new world,
     in which the unity of knowledge,
the nature of human communities,
     the order of society,
the order of ideas,
     the very notions
of society and culture
     have changed, and will not return
to what they have been in the past.

What is new is new
     not because it has never been there before,
but because it has changed in quality.

One thing that is new
     is the prevalence of newness,
the changing scale and scope
     of change itself,
so that the world alters
     as we walk in it,
so that the years of man's life measure
     not some small growth
or rearrangement or moderation
     of what he learned in childhood,
but a great upheaval.

                              Robert Oppenheimer

A new mentality

No generation
has exactly the same mentality
as the generation
that went before.
Christians have continually
to appropriate Christian truth
afresh,
not change but rethink their beliefs
and gain a new understanding
of the revelation of God in Christ.
That revelation is a reality
always present.

Charles Davis

Open to new ways

He felt a quiet manhood,
    non-assertive
but of sturdy and strong blood.
    He knew
that he would no more quail
    before his guides
wherever they should point.
    He had been to touch the great death,
and found that, after all,
    it was but the great death.
He was a man.

It rained.
    The procession
of weary soldiers
    became a bedraggled train,
despondent and muttering,
    marching with churning effort
in a trough of liquid brown mud
    under a low, wretched sky.
Yet the youth smiled,
    for he saw that the world
was a world for him,
    though many discovered it
to be made of oaths and walking sticks.
    He had rid himself
of the red sickness of battle.
    He turned now with a lover's thirst
to images of tranquil skies,
    fresh meadows, cool brooks--
an existence of soft and eternal peace.

Over the river a golden ray of sun
    came through the hosts of leaden rain clouds.

                                    Stephen Crane

Sharing the modern outlook

To be "modern" is not a monopoly of modern man.
　　　There have been modern men in most eras,
and there have been other modern eras.
　　　But . . . no other age has gone so far in the belief
that the spirit of modernity might be widely shared,
　　　and that all men might participate
in the goods and responsibilities
　　　of modern civilization.
The modern spirit in Athens
　　　was a brief and glimmering thing,
arising in a society based on slavery.
　　　The modern spirit in fifteenth-century Italy
was an aristocratic phenomenon, limited to an elite.
　　　But our own revolution of modernity
has led to the unprecedented vision of a society
　　　in which the opportunity for personal achievement
and social power would be generally diffused among men.

Charles Frankel

A new earth being formed

There is a basic Christian vision
    that should color all our thinking:
The earth is building itself for God.
    Mankind is in process toward a promise.
The promise is of a new reality,
    a new earth that is both spiritual
and material.
    This new earth is not
like a bouquet of cut flowers,
    where each flower is put into its
proper place
    by the loving hand of God.
The new earth is like a great tree,
    growing within the divine milieu,
shaping its own destiny.
    Each spring, new buds and leaves appear.
Year by year,
    the shape and purpose of the tree
becomes clearer and more definite.
    Its growth and process is governed
by the vitality and strength
    of the whole tree.
Slowly and laboriously,
    through the action of men and women
who share this vision of mankind,
    the new earth is being formed.

                                        Ruth M. Cullen

LISTEN
TO
LOVE
IN
SUMMER

Summer is a counterpoint of color and candy, of streets and flowers and people.

Summer vibrates with work. Summer is hot and tired and wrinkled. It searches for shade, for a breeze, or for a brook. It waits for the cooling touch of evening.

In summer the Spirit of love comes working itself into people's lives. Love in summer is fire and water. It is the sun that penetrates the body, and the clouds heavy with rain ready to burst upon the earth.

Love in summer is violent and intense. It searches within. People feel things deeply. They spin and weave and knit themselves together.

Love in summer can be happy or sad, impish, flaming, cunning or hesitant and confused. It is a time of tension. But love grows in the heat of it all.

Listen to love in summer.

Love is outgoing

Out into the country

One of the pleasantest things in the world
    is going a journey;
but I like to go by myself.
    I can enjoy society in a room;
but out of doors, nature is company enough for me.
    I am then never less alone
than when alone.

I cannot see the wit of walking
    and talking at the same time.
When I am in the country,
    I wish to vegetate like the country.
I am not for criticizing hedgerows and black cattle.
    I go out of town in order to forget the town
and all that is in it.
    There are those who for this purpose
go to watering places,
    and carry the metropolis with them.
I like more elbowroom,
    and fewer incumbrances.
I like solitude,
    when I give myself up to it,
for the sake of solitude.

William Hazlitt

A man among men

Jesus himself, very different from
    the ascetic John the Baptist,
took part in banquets
    and let himself be abused
as "a glutton and a wine-drinker" (Mt 11:19).
    He set a high value on marriage,
reasserted its indissolubility,
    and was tenderly affectionate
toward children.
    He would not interfere
in property matters,
    and proposed
no new distribution of wealth.
    He accepted the authority
of the state
    and its right
to levy taxes,
    and saw civic duties
in a positive light.

    Nor did Jesus want
to cut his disciples off
    from the world.
He did not want them, like the Essenes,
    to dissociate themselves
from the people and found closed communities
    with a strict moral code.

He sent his disciples out
    into the world.
Peter, the brothers of the Lord
    and the other apostles
took their wives with them
    when they went to preach the Gospel.

                                   Hans Küng

160

To all the people

And he told them, "Go into the whole world
    and proclaim the good news."

Mark 16:15

To me, who am less
    than the least of all God's people,
he has granted of his grace
    the privilege of proclaiming to the gentiles
the good news
    of the unfathomable riches of Christ,
and of bringing to light how this hidden purpose
    was to be put into effect.
It was hidden for long ages
    in God the creator of the universe,
in order that now through the church
    the wisdom of God in all its varied forms
might be made known.
    This is in accord with his age-long purpose
which he achieved in Christ Jesus our Lord.
    In him we have access to God with freedom,
in the confidence born of trust in him.

Ephesians 3:8-12 (NEB)

Love is filled with the Spirit

May the splendor of your brightness
        shine upon us, Lord,
and the light of your Spirit
        strengthen us
who are born again
        through your grace.

Pentecost Prayer

The Spirit of God

When the day of Pentecost had come,
    they were all together in one place.
And suddenly a sound came from heaven
    like the rush of a mighty wind,
and it filled all the house
    where they were sitting.
And there appeared to them
    tongues as of fire,
distributed and resting
    on each one of them.
And they were all filled
    with the Holy Spirit
and began to speak in other tongues,
    as the Spirit gave them utterance.

Acts 2:1-4

That the hearts of men,
    touched by things seen outwardly,
might be turned from the manifestation
    in time of Him
as coming to His hidden eternity
    as ever present.

Saint Augustine

Images of life

Dying was nothing
    and he had no picture of it
nor fear of it in his mind.
    But living was a field of grain
blowing in the wind
    on the side of a hill.
Living was a hawk in the sky.
    Living was an earthen jar of water
and the chaff blowing.
    Living was a horse between your legs
and a carbine under one leg
    and a hill and a valley
and a stream with trees along it
    and the far side of the valley
and the hills beyond.

                              Ernest Hemingway

This is
the day
which the Lord
has made;
let us rejoice
and be glad
in it.

Psalm 118:24

The power of the Spirit

May the God of hope fill you with all joy
        and peace in your faith,
so that through the power of the Holy Spirit
        you may have hope in abundance.

                                    Romans 15:13

He who believes in me
will also do the works that I do;
and greater works than these will he do.

                                    John 14:12

To live in the Spirit

When men belong to Jesus Christ in such a way
    that they have freedom to recognize
his word as addressed also to them,
    his work as done also for them,
the message about him as also their task;
    and then for their part,
freedom to hope for the best
    for all other men,
this happens, indeed,
    as their human experience and action,
and yet not in virtue of their human capacity,
    determination and exertion,
but solely on the basis of the free gift of God
    in which all this is given to them.
In this giving and gift God is the Holy Spirit.
    When we speak of the Holy Spirit,
let us look not at all men,
    but at special men belonging in a special way
to Jesus Christ.
    When we speak of the Holy Spirit,
we have to do with the men who belong
    to Jesus Christ in the special way

that they have the freedom to recognize his Word,
    his work, his message in a definite way
and also to hope on their part the best for all men.
    To have inner ears for the Word of Christ,
to become thankful for his work and at the same time
    responsible for the message about him and, lastly,
to take confidence in men for Christ's sake--
    that is the freedom which we obtain,
when Christ breathes on us,
    when he sends us his Holy Spirit.
If he no longer lives in a historical or heavenly,
    a theological or ecclesiastical remoteness from me,
if he approaches me and takes possession of me,
    the result will be that I hear,
that I am thankful and responsible
    and that finally I may hope for myself
and for all others; in other words,
    that I may live in a Christian way.
It is a tremendously big thing
    and by no means a matter of course,
to obtain freedom.
    We do not "have" this freedom;
it is again and again given to us by God.

                                        Karl Barth

A child in the sun

The thief comes only to steal
        and kill and destroy;
I came that they may have life,
        and have it abundantly.

                                        John 10:10

By health I mean the power to live a full,
        adult, living, breathing life
in close contact with what I love--
        the earth and the wonders thereof--
the sea, the sun.
        All that we mean when we speak
of the eternal world.
        I want to enter into it,
to be part of it, to live in it,
        to learn from it, to lose all
that is superficial and acquired in me
        and to become a conscious direct
human being.
        I want, by understanding myself,
to understand others.
        I want to be all that I am capable
of becoming so that I may be
        a *child in the sun*.

Warm, eager, living life--
        to be rooted in life--
to learn, to desire to know,
        to feel, to think, to act.
That is what I want.

                                        Katherine Mansfield

A higher freedom

Freedom is the necessary condition
    of happiness
as well as of virtue;
    freedom, not in the sense
of the ability to make
    arbitrary choices
and not freedom from necessity,
    but freedom to realize
that which one potentially is,
    to fulfill the true
nature of man
    according to the laws
of his existence.

Erich Fromm

To transform the profane

One of the great things
    that is happening
in the Church today is--
    we're beginning
to find out
    that maybe
what we call secular
    is also part
of the sacred
    and that the only way
to get anything sacred
    short of God
is to transform
    the profane.

Bernard Cooke

To see many things

Whoever seeks to gain his life will lose it,
    but whoever loses his life will preserve it.

Luke 17:33

"When someone is seeking," said Siddhartha,
    "it happens quite easily
that he only sees the thing that he is seeking;
    that he is unable to find anything,
unable to absorb anything,
    because he is only thinking of the thing
he is seeking,
    because he has a goal,
because he is obsessed with his goal.
    Seeking means: to have a goal;
but finding means: to be free,
    to be receptive, to have no goal.
You, O worthy one, are perhaps indeed a seeker,
    for in striving towards your goal,
you do not see many things that are under your nose."

Hermann Hesse

To see nothing

They have mouths, but do not speak;
    eyes, but do not see.
They have ears, but do not hear;
    noses, but do not smell.
They have hands, but do not feel;
    feet, but do not walk;
and they do not make a sound
    in their throat.
Those who make them are like them;
    so are all who trust in them.

Psalm 115:5-8

Love
means
doing
things

Act on the message

Only be sure that you act on the message
    and not merely listen; for that would
be to mislead yourselves. A man who listens
    to the message but never acts upon it
is like one who looks in a mirror at the
    face nature gave him. He glances at
himself and goes away, and at once forgets
    what he looked like. But the man who
looks closely into the perfect law, the
    law that makes us free, and who lives
in its company, does not forget what he
    hears, but acts upon it; and that is
the man who by acting will find happiness.

James 1:22-25 (NEB)

Doing something to help mankind

So there I sat and smoked my cigar until I lapsed into thought. Among other thoughts I remember these:

"You are going on," I said to myself, "to become an old man, without being anything, and without really undertaking to do anything.

"On the other hand, wherever you look about you, in literature and in life, you see the celebrated names and figures, the precious and much heralded men who are coming into prominence and are much talked about, the many benefactors of the age who know how to benefit mankind by making life easier and easier. And what are you doing?"

Here my soliloquy was interrupted, for my cigar was smoked out and a new one had to be lit. So I smoked again, and then suddenly this thought flashed through my mind:

"You must do something, but inasmuch as with your limited capacities it will be impossible to make anything easier than it has become, you must, with the same humanitarian enthusiasm as the others, undertake to make something harder."

This notion pleased me immensely ... For when all combine in every way to make everything easier, there remains only one possible danger, namely, that the ease becomes so great that it becomes altogether too great; then there is only one want left, though it is not yet a felt want, when people will want difficulty.

Out of love for mankind, and out of despair at my embarrassing situation, seeing that I had accomplished nothing and was unable to make anything easier than it had already been made, and moved by genuine interest in those who make everything easy, I conceived it as my task to create difficulties.

Sören Kierkegaard

To be sure he sees all the possibilities

I just want him to stay with me till I can be sure
        he won't turn into *Norman Nothing.* I want
to be sure he'll know when he's chickening out
        on himself. I want him to get to know
exactly the special thing he is or else
        he won't notice it when it starts to go.
I want him to stay awake and know who the
        phonies are. I want him to know how to
holler and put up an argument, I want a little
        guts to show before I can let him go.
I want to be sure he sees all the wild possibilities.
        I want him to know it's worth all the trouble
just to give the world a little nudge when you
        get the chance. And I want him to know the
subtle, sneaky, important reason why he was born
        a human being and not a chair.

                                        Herb Gardner

182

Only playing a game

At times he heard within him a soft, gentle voice,
    which reminded him quietly, complained quietly,
so that he could hardly hear it.
    Then he suddenly saw clearly
that he was leading a strange life,
    that he was doing many things that were only a game,
that he was quite cheerful and sometimes experienced
        pleasure,
    but that real life was flowing past him
and did not touch him.
    Like a player who plays with his ball,
he played with his business, with the people around him,
    watched them, derived amusement from them;
but with his heart, with his real nature,
    he was not there.
His real self wandered elsewhere, far away,
    wandered on and on invisibly
and had nothing to do with his life.

                                        Hermann Hesse

Trying to "be good"

They were trying to guide us
    to do right and be good,
and they didn't even know
    what being good was.
When I was a little boy,
    Mama and Dad would beat me
and tell me, "You better be good,"
    but I didn't know what being good was.
To me, it meant that they just wanted me
    to sit down and fold my hands
or something crazy like that.
    Stay in front of the house,
don't go anyplace,
    don't get into trouble.
I didn't know what it meant,
    and I don't think
they knew what it meant,
    because they couldn't ever tell me
what they really wanted.

The way I saw it,
everything I was doing was good.
    If I stole something
and didn't get caught,
    I was good.
If I got into a fight with somebody
    I tried to be good
and beat him.
    If I broke into a place,
I tried to be quiet and steal
    as much as I could.
I was always trying to be good.

Claude Brown

Results are obtained by exploiting
    opportunities, not by solving
problems. All one can hope to get
    by solving a problem is to
restore normality.
    The pertinent question is not
how to do things right but how to
    find the right things to do,
and to concentrate resources and
    efforts on them.

Peter F. Drucker

The son who obeyed

"But what do you think about this?
      A man had two sons.
He went to the first and said,
      'My boy, go and work today in the vineyard.'
'I will, sir,' the boy replied;
      but he never went.
The father came to the second
      and said the same.
'I will not,' he replied, but afterwards
      he changed his mind and went.
Which of these two did as his father wished?"

"The second," they said.

Then Jesus answered, "I tell you this:
      tax-gatherers and prostitutes
are entering the kingdom of God
      ahead of you.
For when John came to show you
      the right way to live,
you did not believe him,
      but the tax-gatherers and prostitutes did;
and even when you had seen that,
      you did not change your minds
and believe him."

Matthew 21:28-32 (NEB)

Transforming the patterns of life

If we are going to become involved in transforming
        not just the lives of individuals
but the patterns of human living, we must start
        transforming the patterns of communication,
of recreation, of government, of professional life.
        To work at this level, we obviously need,
in addition to an accurate understanding of Christianity,
        a deep professional understanding of these areas.
We cannot be ignorant of social structures
        and have any hope of changing them;
we cannot have any impact in a given profession unless
        we are recognized as competent within that profession.
The involved Christian, then, has
        as a necessary dictate of his apostolic life
the gaining of two kinds of knowledge,
        two kinds of understanding,
which he must bring together.
        Only if he understands deeply what the faith is
can he infuse it into these patterns of life;
        but only if he understands these patterns
can he show others what Christ and the Church
        are meant to do in the world of men.

Bernard Cooke

Here are words
you may trust,
words that merit
full acceptance:
"With this before us
we labor and struggle,
because we have set
our hope
on the living God,
who is the savior
of all men"--
the savior,
above all,
of believers.

1 Timothy 4:9-10 (NEB)

Love learns

If you love me and keep my commandments, then at my request the Father will give you another Paraclete to be with you forever--the Spirit of Truth. The world cannot accept him because it neither sees nor recognizes him; but you can recognize him because he remains with you and will be within you.

John 14:15-17

Discovery

I cannot invent
New things,
Like the airships
Which sail
On silver wings;
But today
A wonderful thought
In the dawn was given,
And the stripes of my robe,
Shining from wear,
Were suddenly fair,
Bright with a light
Falling from heaven--
Gold, and silver, and bronze
Lights from the windows of Heaven.

And the thought
Was this:
That a secret plan
Is hid in my hand;
That my hand is big,
Big,
Because of this plan.

That God,
Who dwells in my hand,
Knows this secret plan
Of the things He will do for the world
Using my hand!

Toyohiko Kagawa

Discovering reality

The word which the Greeks used for truth is
    "aletheia," which means discovery,
to take away the veil that covers and hides a thing.
    Facts cover up reality: while we are
in the midst of their innumerable swarmings
    we are in chaos and confusion.
In order to discover reality we must
    for a moment lay aside the facts
that surge about us, and remain alone with our minds.
    Then, on our own risk and account,
we imagine a reality. We construct an imaginary reality.
    We . . . compare those facts which
the imagined reality would produce with the actual facts
    which surround us.
If they mate happily one with another,
    we have discovered the reality which the facts
covered and kept secret.

                                        José Ortega y Gasset

Accepting the facts

The past weeks have been more of a strain
      than anything I have been through before.
But it cannot be altered.
      It is always more difficult
to adapt oneself to something
      which might have been altered
than it is to the inevitable.
      But once facts have taken shape
they must simply be accepted.
      What I am thinking of most today
is that you too will soon be facing facts
      which will be really hard for you,
probably harder than for me.
      I think we ought to do all in our power
to alter these facts while there is still time,
      and then when all our efforts have
proved fruitless it becomes much easier
      to endure them.
Of course, not everything that happens
      is the will of God, yet in the last resort
nothing happens without his will.

Dietrich Bonhoeffer

Knowledge

The one and only resource of any business:
    knowledge.
Knowledge is a specifically human resource.
    It is not found in books.
Books contain information.
    Knowledge is the ability
to apply information
    to specific work
and performance.

Peter F. Drucker

Finding meaning

How many times have we seen people leave work
    that they care deeply about
to do something that does not interest them
    because it will bring more money
or higher status or greater power?
    How many times have we seen middle-aged people
caught in a pattern of activities
    they don't care about at all--
playing bridge with people they don't really like,
    going to cocktail parties that bore them,
doing things because "it's the thing to do."
    Such people would be refreshed
and renewed if they could wipe the slate clean
    and do *one little thing*
that they really cared about deeply,
    one little thing that they could do
with burning conviction.

John W. Gardner

To know Jesus Christ

And just because as Christians
     we may live in the truth of Jesus Christ
and therefore in the light
     of the knowledge of God
and therefore with an illumined reason,
     we shall also become sure
of the meaning of our own existence
     and of the ground and goal
of all that happens.

To know Him is to know all.
     To be touched and gripped
by the Spirit in this realm
     means being led into all truth.
If a man believes and knows God,
     he can no longer ask,
What is the meaning of my life?
     But by believing
he actually lives the meaning of his life.

Karl Barth

To know the mind of the Lord

The Spirit reaches the depths of everything,
 even the depths of God.
After all, the depths of a man
 can only be known by his own spirit,
not by any other man,
 and in the same way the depths of God
can only be known by the Spirit of God.

As scripture says:
 Who can know the mind of the Lord,
so who can teach him?
 But we are those
who have the mind of Christ.

1 Corinthians 2:10-11, 16 (JB)

O the depth of the riches and wisdom
 and knowledge of God!
How insearchable are his judgments
 and how inscrutable his ways!
"For who has known the mind of the Lord,
 or who has been his counselor?"

Romans 11:33-34

No one has ever seen God;
 it is the only Son,
who is nearest to the Father's heart,
 who has made him known.

John 1:18 (JB)

Partial knowledge

Our knowledge and our prophecy alike are partial,
and the partial vanishes when wholeness comes.

When I was a child, my speech, my outlook and my thoughts
were all childish. When I grew up, I had finished with
childish things.

Now we see only puzzling reflections in a mirror, but then
we shall see face to face. My knowledge now is partial;
then it will be whole, like God's knowledge of me.

1 Corinthians 13:9-12 (NEB)

Love searches within

The search for self

All insight into the meaning
        or even existence of a "self"
comes from the experience
        of the self in relation.

This is why the teaching of Christ
        not only stresses the necessity
of search for the Kingdom of Heaven
        but makes it equally clear
that the area of the search,
        wherever else it may be,
is primarily that of relations
        between people.
It is the opposite of those philosophies
        which stress detachment
from human contacts and desires.
        In Christ's view
there is to be no withdrawal
        into communion with the source of life
if that means withdrawal from people;
        in fact he makes ordinary,
concrete, down-to-earth usefulness
        to other people the test
of the reality of any man's search
        for truth.

Rosemary Haughton

The personal attraction of grace

God, then, works within man,
     and the soul
in its innermost depths
     experiences his action,
which is both
     illumination and inspiration,
a summons of light and love.
     It is grace
which enlightens and attracts--
     and this is perfectly true;
but it means that *God himself,*
     in his personal reality,
enlightens and attracts us
     by his grace.
It is not the action
     of a blind force,
an impassive sun
     shedding light
without discrimination.
     It is a Person,
who is light and love,
     who gives a little of himself
to a person in need,
     one who craves
that light and love.

Jean Mouroux

My neighbor

Sam was walking along the street
    and a bum approached him for money.
Sam is like so many;
    each time a derelict asks for a dime,
he feels a coward if he pays the money,
    and is ashamed if he doesn't.
This once, Sam happened to think,
    I will not be bullied, and hurried past.
But the bum was not to be lost so easily.
    "Have a heart, Jack," he called after
in a whiskey voice, "I need a drink bad."
    Sam stopped, Sam began to laugh.
"Just so it isn't for coffee,
    here's a quarter," he said,
and he laughed, and the bum laughed.
    "You're a man's man," the bum said.
Sam went away pleased with himself,
    thinking about such things
as the community which existed between all people.
    It was cheap of Sam.
He should know better.
    He should know he was merely relieved
the situation had turned out so well.
    Although he thinks he is sorry for bums,
Sam really hates them.
    Who knows what violence they can offer?

Norman Mailer

A crisis of the heart

The crisis of our time, as we are beginning
    slowly and painfully to perceive,
is a crisis not of the hands
    but of the hearts.
It is a crisis of hunger--but not a crisis
    created by any doubt as to our ability
to feed ourselves. It is a crisis of cold--
    but not a crisis of cold created
by any doubt as to our ability
    to put roofs over our heads
or clothes on our backs.
    The failure is a failure of desire.
It is because we the people do not wish--
    because we the people do not know
what it is that we should wish--
    because we the people do not know
what kind of world we should imagine,
    that this trouble haunts us.
The failure is a failure of the spirit:
    a failure of the spirit to imagine,
a failure of the spirit to imagine and desire.

                    Archibald MacLeish

The Spirit
reaches the depths of everything,
even the depths of God.
After all, the depths of a man
can only be known by his own spirit,
not by any other man,
and in the same way
the depths of God
can only be known
by the Spirit of God.

1 Corinthians 2:10-11 (JB)

Love lives with conflict

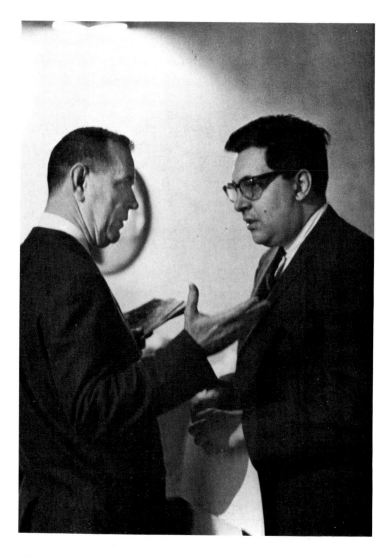

Conflict between persons

The inevitability of conflict between persons
        rests on the fact
that being means power
        and power implies otherness
and opposition.
        To be at all is to be powerful,
to have the capacity to meet resistance successfully,
        to be able to stand up to otherness.
In the absence of resistance,
        not only does a given amount of power
remain untested and undefined:
        it is completely lacking in meaning.
The problem of community,
        which is the form of personal life,
is the one of deciding on whose terms
        it shall be lived.
Simply to impose my terms on the other person
        is to deny his freedom and responsibility;
simply to accept his terms without demur
        is to abandon my own.
In either case, there is no community
        but a kind of fusion or absorption instead.
For community implies a mutuality
        of distinct initiatives as an ongoing project.
Love without power is not enough,
        because love without power soon ceases to be love.
Without the strength to resist encroachments,
        openness to the other comes down simply
to "giving in." The person, then,
        is called to do battle;
there is no advance without it.
        If he is also called to know peace,
it is because peace is not a state but a process,
        not just a matter of avoiding conflicts
but of keeping our conflicts constructive.

                                        Robert O. Johann

The points at issue

If you come at me with your fists doubled,
    I think I can promise you
that mine will double as fast as yours;
    but if you come to me and say,
"Let us sit down and take counsel together,
    and, if we differ from one another,
understand just what the points at issue are,"
    we will presently find that we are not
so far apart after all,
    that the points on which we differ are few
and the points on which we agree are many.

                                        Woodrow Wilson

Nothing can come between us

Nothing therefore can come between us and the love of Christ, even if we are troubled or worried, or being persecuted, or lacking food or clothes, or being threatened or even attacked.

For I am certain of this: neither death nor life, no angel, no prince, nothing that exists, nothing still to come, not any power, or height or depth, nor any created thing, can ever come between us and the love of God made visible in Christ Jesus our Lord.

Romans 8:35, 38-39 (JB)

Let the spirit flow forth

We men are impenetrable. Spirits,
    like solid bodies, can only
communicate with one another by the
        contact of their surfaces, not
by penetrating one another, still less
        by fusing together.
You have heard me say a thousand times
        that most spirits seem to me like
crustaceans, with the bone outside and
        the flesh inside. And when in
some books that I have forgotten I read
        what a painful and terrible thing
it would be if the human spirit were
        to be incarcerated in a crab and
had to make use of a crab's senses,
        organs, and members, I said to myself:
"This is what actually happens;
        we are all unfortunate crabs,
shut up in hard shells."
        And this is why I believe that it is
necessary to agitate the masses, to shake
        men and winnow them as in a sieve,
to throw them against one another, in
        order to see if in this way
their shells will not break and their
        spirits flow forth, whether they
will not mingle and unite with one another.

Miguel de Unamuno

For my part I always try to meet everyone
    half-way, regarding not my own good
but the good of the many, so that they may be
    saved. Follow my example as I follow Christ's.

1 Corinthians 10:33

Never lose heart

There was once a judge who cared nothing
        for God or man, and in the same town
there was a widow who constantly came before him
        demanding justice against her opponent.
For a long time he refused; but in the end
        he said to himself, "True, I care nothing
for God or man; but this widow is so great
        a nuisance that I will see her righted
before she wears me out with her persistence."

The Lord said, "You hear what the unjust judge says;
        and will not God vindicate his chosen,
who cry out to him day and night,
        while he listens patiently to them?
I tell you, he will vindicate them soon enough.

Luke 18:2-8 (NEB)

217

Love is courage

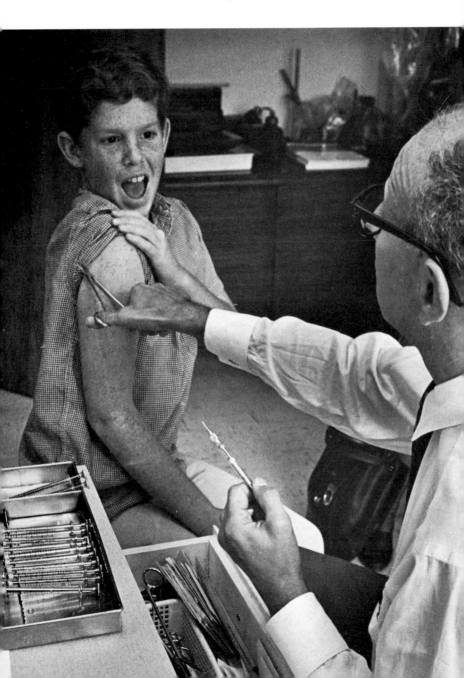

The test of courage

The great impediment to action is,
    in our opinion, not discussion,
but the want of that knowledge
    which is gained by discussion
preparatory to action.
    For we have a peculiar power
of thinking before we act
    and of acting too,
whereas other men are courageous
    from ignorance,
but hesitate upon reflection.
    And they are surely
to be esteemed the bravest spirits who,
    having the clearest sense
both of the pains and the pleasures
    of life,
do not on that account
    shrink from danger.

Thucydides

Overcoming fear

He had done it too many times in his imagination.
    Too many times he had seen the horns,
seen the bull's wet muzzle, the ear twitching,
    then the head go down and the charge,
the hoofs thudding and the hot bull pass him
    as he swung the cape,
to re-charge as he swung the cape again,
    then again, and again, and again,
to end winding the bull around him
    in his great media-veronica,
and walk swingingly away, with bull hairs
    caught in the gold ornaments of his jacket
from the close passes; the bull standing
    hypnotized and the crowd applauding.
No, he would not be afraid.
    Even if he ever was afraid
he knew that he could do it anyway.
    He had confidence. "I wouldn't be afraid,"
he said.

Ernest Hemingway

Caught in a storm

The rain poured on him, flowed, drove in sheets.
    He breathed in gasps; and sometimes the water
he swallowed was fresh and sometimes it was salt.
    For the most part he kept his eyes shut tight,
as if suspecting his sight might be destroyed in
    the immense flurry of the elements. When he
ventured to blink hastily, he derived some moral
    support from the green gleam of the starboard
light shining feebly upon the flight of rain and
    sprays. He saw the head of the wave topple
over, adding the might of its crash to the tremendous
    uproar raging around him. After a crushing
thump on his back he found himself suddenly afloat
    and borne upwards. He concluded himself gone
overboard. All the time he was being tossed, flung,
    and rolled in great volumes of water, he kept
on repeating mentally, with the utmost precipitation,
    the words : "My God! My God! My God!"

Joseph Conrad

To meet whatever comes

We ask God that you may receive from him
    all wisdom and spiritual understanding
for full insight into his will,
    so that your manner of life may be
worthy of the Lord and entirely pleasing to him.
    We pray that you may bear fruit
in active goodness of every kind,
    and grow in the knowledge of God.
May he strengthen you in his glorious might,
    with ample power to meet whatever comes
with fortitude, patience and joy;
    and to give thanks to the Father
who has made you fit to share
    the heritage of God's people
in the realm of light.

Colossians 1:9-12 (NEB)

Therefore do not be anxious about tomorrow,
    for tomorrow will be anxious for itself.
Let the day's own trouble
    be sufficient for the day.

Matthew 6:34

224

Risks

There are essentially four kinds of risk:
The risk one must accept.
  The risk one can afford to take.
The risk one cannot afford to take.
  The risk one cannot afford not to take.

Peter F. Drucker

The kingdom of heaven is like a merchant
    in search of fine pearls,
who, on finding one pearl of great value,
    went and sold all that he had
        and bought it.

Matthew 13:45-46

Behold, I have given you authority
    to tread upon serpents and scorpions,
and over all the power of the enemy;
    and nothing shall hurt you.

Luke 10:19

For those who see

Earth's crammed with heaven
And every common bush afire with God;
And only he who sees takes off his shoes--
The rest sit round it and pluck blackberries.

Elizabeth Barrett Browning

To master or be mastered

Man either masters and manages his environment
    or he is mastered and managed by it.
The call to freedom is at the same time
    a call to responsibility.
In terms of modern urban life this means
    that we should never seriously ask
"Is New York City governable?"
    or "Can nuclear war be prevented?"
or "Can racial justice be achieved?"
    Man is placed in an environment
of problems which he is called to master.
    God has not stacked the cards against man
the way fate does in Greek tragedy
    or a Thomas Hardy novel.
To believe the kerygma is to believe
    that man not only *should* but *can*
"have dominion over the earth."
    For the Bible, there are no powers anywhere
which are not essentially tameable
    and ultimately humanizable.
To deny this, in word or deed,
    is to "worship the creature
rather than the Creator," to open the door
    and readmit the banished furies,
to genuflect before some faceless Kismet.

                                        Harvey Cox

To believe the heart

O world, thou choosest not the better part!
It is not wisdom to be only wise,
And on the inward vision close the eyes,
But it is wisdom to believe the heart.
Columbus found a world, and had no chart,
Save one that faith deciphered in the skies;
To trust the soul's invincible surmise
Was all his science and his only art.

Our knowledge is a torch of smoky pine
That lights the pathway but one step ahead
Across a void of mystery and dread.
Bid, then, the tender light of faith to shine
By which alone the mortal heart is led
Unto the thinking of the thought divine.

George Santayana

Blessed is the man who trusts in the Lord,
whose trust is the Lord.
He is like a tree planted by water,
that sends out its roots by the stream,
and does not fear when heat comes,
for its leaves remain green,
and is not anxious in the year of drought,
for it does not cease to bear fruit.

Jeremiah 17:7-10

Love
finds
love

Man and woman

Then the Lord God said,
    "It is not good that man is alone;
I will make him a helper
    like himself."
The Lord God cast the man
    into a deep sleep and, while he slept,
took one of his ribs and closed up
    its place with flesh.
And the rib which the Lord God
    took from the man, he made into a woman,
and brought her to him.
    Then the man said, "She now is
bone of my bones, and flesh of my flesh;
    she shall be called Woman,
for from man she has been taken."
    For this reason a man leaves his father
and mother, and clings to his wife,
    and the two become one flesh.

Genesis 2:18, 21-24

Together we are a mystery

I swim by your side
    in the warm, clear water,
I wait for you to appear
    in the doorway
under the wisteria.
    You say "Good morning" to me,
and I know your dreams,
    your first thoughts
on the fringes of sleep--
    and yet you are a mystery.

We talk:
    your voice, your thoughts,
and the word you use
    to express them
are the most familiar
    in the world to me.
Each of us can end a sentence
    begun by the other.
And you are--
    and we are--
a mystery.

Anne Philipe

A shy friend

My longing to talk to someone became so intense
    that somehow or other
I took it into my head to choose Peter.

Sometimes... I tried to think of an excuse
    to stay in his room and get him talking,
without it being too noticeable,
    and my chance came yesterday.
Peter has a mania for crossword puzzles
    at the moment
and hardly does anything else.
    I helped him with them
and we soon sat opposite each other
    at his table,
he on the chair and me on the divan.
    It gave me a queer feeling
each time I looked into his deep blue eyes,
    and... I noticed his shy manner
and it made me feel very gentle;
    I couldn't refrain from meeting
those dark eyes again and again,
    and with my whole heart
I almost beseeched him:
    Oh, tell me, what is going on inside you,
oh, can't you look beyond this ridiculous chatter?

Anne Frank

To be loved in return

In the mystery of social love
        there is found the realization
of "the other"
        not only as one to be loved by us,
so that we may perfect ourselves,
        but also as one who can become
more perfect by loving us.
        The vocation to charity
is a call not only
        to love but to *be loved.*
The man who does not care at all
        whether or not he is loved
is ultimately unconcerned
        about the true welfare
of the other and of society.
        Hence we cannot love
unless we also consent
        to be loved in return.

Thomas Merton

A Kind of Loving

I sing songs for people I can't have
people I meet once and will never see again.
It is for me a kind of loving.
A kind of loving, for me.

I make words for people I've not met
those who will not turn to follow after me.
It is for me a kind of loving.
A kind of loving, for me.

Rod McKuen

The attitude of love

Love is not primarily a relationship
    to a specific person;
it is an attitude,
    an orientation of character
which determines the relatedness
    of a person
to the world as a whole,
    not toward one "object" of love.
If a person loves only one other person
    and is indifferent to the rest of his fellow men,
his love is not love
    but a selfish attachment, or an enlarged egotism.
Yet, most people believe that love
    is constituted by the object,
not by the faculty.
    In fact, they even say
that it is a proof of the intensity
    of their love
when they do not love anybody
    but the "loved" person.

                                        Erich Fromm

A new air of freedom

In love,
    the gates of my soul spring open,
allowing me to breathe a new air of freedom
    and forget my own petty self.
In love, my whole being streams forth
    out of the rigid confines of
narrowness and self-assertion,
which makes me a prisoner of
my own poverty and emptiness.

Karl Rahner

Two are better than one

Two are better than one, because they have
    a good reward for their toil.
For if they fall, one will lift up his fellow;
    but woe to him who is alone
when he falls and has not another
    to lift him up. Again, if two
lie together, they are warm;
    but how can one be warm alone?
And though a man might prevail
    against one who is alone, two will
        withstand him.
A threefold cord is not quickly broken.

Ecclesiastes 4:9-12

Love faces refusal and separation

Afraid to lose

Man is a being who does not dare
    to complete himself.
He loves loving,
    but he is afraid to sacrifice;
he loves giving,
    but he is afraid to lose.
He enjoys his independence,
    he cultivates
his autonomous self,
    but he soon finds it
oppressively sterile and monotonous.
    He wants to take the risk of loving,
but he is torn with anxiety
    when he feels that one cannot
at the same time
    give oneself and keep oneself,
to do the will of another
    and continue to live according
to one's own.

                                        Louis Evely

The unloved ones

Americans like to believe that dreams come true.
    We are a dream nation; everybody wins.
No one has bothered to make a count
    of the severest losers, those children
stricken with the disease that does not show,
    those utterly discarded,
literally cast away from human warmth,
    left on doorsteps, benches, in churches,
subway trains and garbage pails.
    They are the loveless almost beyond redemption;
the comforting arms of teachers, social workers
    and nuns cannot heal the scars.
These children can be seen
    in the orphanages and foundling homes,
some left by destitute parents,
    others simply abandoned;
everyone tries hard to bring back to them
    that which seems lost forever.

Norman Rosten

Refusing to share

What is true of all free, personal relationships
     is preeminently true of the relation of God and man.
There is the possibility that despite
     a successful start one partner may refuse
to give and may turn in upon himself
     and away from the other.
From the first moment of their dialogue
     God knew the weakness of man.
He knew that despite all his testimonies
     of love and fidelity
man would draw back
     and prefer to take a path that seemed easier.

Gabriel Moran

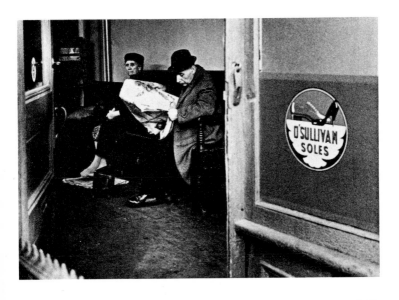

Not always sure

How can we be sure of anything
    the tide changes.
The wind that made the grain wave gently yesterday
    blows down the trees tomorrow.
And the sea sends sailors crashing on the rocks,
    as easily as it guides them safely home.
        I love the sea
but it doesn't make me less afraid of it.
        I love you
but I'm not always sure of what you are
    and how you feel.

Rod McKuen

Separation from those we love

Nothing can fill the gap when we are away
        from those we love, and it would be wrong
to try and find anything. We must simply
        hold out and win through. That sounds
very hard at first, but at the same time
        it is a great consolation, since leaving
the gap unfilled preserves the bonds between us.
        It is nonsense to say that God fills the gap;
he does not fill it, but keeps it empty
        so that our communion with another
may be kept alive, even at the cost of pain.

Dietrich Bonhoeffer

The lesson

The Lord said,
"Say, 'We'";
But I shook my head,
Hid my hands tight behind my back, and said,
Stubbornly,
"I."

The Lord said,
"Say, 'We'";
But I looked upon them, grimy and all awry.
Myself in all those twisted shapes? Ah, no!
Distastefully I turned my head away,
Persisting,
"They."

The Lord said,
"Say, 'We'";
And I
At last,
Richer by a hoard
Of years
And tears,
Looked in their eyes and formed the heavy word
That bent my neck and lowed my head:
Like a shamed schoolboy then I mumbled low,
"We,
Lord."

Karle Wilson Baker

Love unites

Something greater than ourselves

Some persons choose to spend their lives
     sharing in a human project more enduring
than themselves. The project shapes their attitudes
     and feelings with a new purpose.
With the project comes a new taste of reality
     and the discovery that there are others
who share the same outlook. There is a feeling
     of strength and solidarity in this experience
that the reality of faith cannot provide.
     To move, on the level of feelings,
from the reality of experience to that of faith
     can be terrifying and bewildering.
But it is in this very movement toward faith
     that persons are called upon to affirm
their trust and joy in being part of
     something greater than themselves.

Diane Plummer

Many faces

The commonest things of nature have qualities
    and characteristics which are stupendous.
They are a revelation to the persons
    who study and analyze them.
Most people, however, find only strange
    and unusual things worth wondering about,
while they take ordinary things for granted.

Consider human faces, for example.
    Anyone who takes a moment to think
will realize the marvelous fact
    that human faces are, at the same time,
very much alike and yet very different.
    Among the vast numbers of men and women on earth,
every human face is like every other human face
    and there is no difficulty
in distinguishing the human species
    from that of the rest of the animals.
At the same time, every human face
    is unlike every other face
and there is no difficulty in telling one person
    from another.
We say that faces are all alike,
    and yet we find them all different.
We should expect all faces to look alike,
    since all persons share the same human nature.
Variety is the real surprise, finding all faces different.

Saint Augustine

Enter into dialogue

Year by year
      the influence
of world-wide communication
      and the growth
in the complexity
      of society
make objectified revelation
      more of a force
to be reckoned with.
      Objective elements
from revelation
      have become diffused
over the world
      and embedded
in the structure of society.
      There is today
practically no one
      to whom Christianity
can deliver
      the message
completely anew.
      Christianity
must acknowledge
      the possibility
of learning something
      of herself
from other religions.
      With all men
and with all religions
      the Church today
must enter into dialogue.

Gabriel Moran

Light is for sharing

"No one lights a lamp and puts it in a cellar,
    but rather on the lamp-stand
so that those who enter may see the light.
    The lamp of your body is the eye.
When your eyes are sound,
    you have light for your whole body;
but when the eyes are bad, you are in darkness.
    See to it then that the light you have
is not darkness,
    it will all be as bright
as when a lamp flashes its rays upon you."

Luke 11:33-36 (NEB)

But light is for communication.
    "Let your light so shine before men
that they may see your good works
    and glorify your Father who is in heaven."
In terms of ordinary living
    this means that if you are really looking
for truth, your own discoveries about it
    will affect your behavior,
will make you 'clearer' to other people
    so that they will see the point
of being committed to something
    more than getting through life
from day to day
    without actual harm or misery,
and will be encouraged in their own efforts.
    Light, in fact,
is essentially a communal thing;
    it is of its nature to be shared.

Rosemary Haughton

The visible Church

Since here and there
        through the Holy Spirit
men meet with Jesus Christ
        and so also with one another,
Christian community visibly arises
        and exists here and there.
It is a form of the one, holy,
        universal people of God
and a communion of holy men and works,
        in that it submits to sole rule
by Jesus Christ,
        in whom it is founded,
that it also aims to live solely
        in the fulfillment of its service
as ambassador,
        that it recognizes its goal solely
in its hope, which is its limit.

Today there is rather too much
        than too little said about the Church.
There is something better:
        let us *be* the Church!

By men assembling...
        in the Holy Spirit
there arises here and there
        a visible Christian congregation.
It is best not to apply
        the idea of invisibility
to the Church; we are all inclined
        to slip away with that in the direction of
some sort of cloud-cuckooland,
        in which the Christians are united
inwardly and invisibly,
        while the visible Church is devalued.

Karl Barth

Different tasks

The gifts we possess differ as they are
      allotted to us by God's grace, and
must be exercised accordingly: the gift
      of inspired utterance, for example,
in proportion to a man's faith; or the
      gift of administration, in administration.
A teacher should employ his gift in teaching,
      and one who has the gift of stirring speech
should use it to stir his hearers. If you give
      to charity, give with all your heart;
if you are a leader, exert yourself to lead,
      if you are helping others in distress,
do it cheerfully.

Romans 12:6-8 (NEB)

A community of believers

The whole body of believers
    was united in heart and soul.
Not a man of them
    claimed any of his possessions
as his own,
    but everything was held in common,
while the apostles bore witness
    with great power
to the resurrection of the Lord Jesus.
    They were all held in high esteem;
for they had never a needy person
    among them,
because all who had property
    in land or houses sold it,
brought the proceeds of the sale,
    and laid the money at the feet
of the apostles;
    it was then distributed
to any one who stood in need.

Acts 4:32-35 (NEB)

For just as the body is one
    and has many members,
and all the members of the body,
    though many, are one body,
so it is with Christ.

1 Corinthians 12:12

A universal love

If I truly love one person,
    I love all persons,
    I love the world,
    I love life.
If I can say to somebody else,
    "I love you,"
I must be able to say,
    "I love in you everybody,
    I love through you the world,
    I love in you also myself."

Erich Fromm

Man, however, is not a self-sufficient
    separate entity,
but is constituted by the things
    he makes his own.
In every form of his being
    man is related to something
other than himself.

If he makes himself the immediate object
  of his efforts,
he is on his last and perilous path;
    for it is possible
that in doing so he will lose
    the Being of the other
and then no longer find anything
    in himself.

Karl Jaspers

One World

And God blessed them,
and God said to them,
"Be fruitful and multiply,
and fill the earth
and subdue it;
and have dominion
over the fish of the sea
and over the birds of the air
and over every living thing
that moves upon the earth."

Genesis 1:28

The promise of new things

From this time forth
I make you hear new things,
              hidden things
which you have not known.

Isaiah 48:6

"Things beyond our seeing,
     things beyond our hearing,
things beyond our imagining,
     all prepared by God
for those who love him,"
     these it is that God
has revealed to us
     through the Spirit.

1 Corinthians 2:9-10 (NEB)

LISTEN
TO
LOVE
IN
AUTUMN

Autumn is melons and mists, purple grapes that cling to the vine and cornstalks that soldier the fields. It is thanksgiving. There is dancing and laughter beneath a magic orange moon. In autumn the world wears well.

Love in autumn is a rich king.

It is harvest time. Relaxed afternoon shadows are long and lean. The sweat and toil and struggling is over. The promise spring made long ago now vibrates with reality. The spirit of love has done his work and mankind is together, united with him. Love is filled to overflowing.

Love in autumn is not afraid of death. The spirit of love sweeps like a wind through the world and whispers in the heart of mankind a higher hope. The earth too feels this hope and tastes its deep flavor. Everything is excited with anticipation.

Listen to love in autumn.

Love gives thanks

Harvest

The threshing floors shall be full of grain,
    the vats shall overflow with wine and oil.
I will restore to you the years
    which the swarming locust has eaten,
the hopper, the destroyer, and the cutter,
    my great army, which I sent among you.
You shall eat in plenty and be satisfied,
    and praise the name of the Lord your God,
who has dealt wondrously with you.
    And my people shall never again be put to shame.

Joel 2:24-26

The music of the autumn winds

The music of the autumn winds sings low,
Down by the ruins of the painted hills,
Where death lies flaming with a marvelous glow,
Upon the ash of rose and daffodils.
But I can find no melancholy here
To see the naked rocks and thinning trees;
Earth strips to grapple with the winter year--
I see her gnarled hills plan for victories!

Edwin Curran

Aware of God's gifts

Almighty God, Father of mercy, we thank you
    for all your goodness and loving kindness
to us and to all mankind.
    You create us, keep us and bless us
in this life.
    You showed your love for use above all,
by redeeming the world in Jesus Christ.
    You bring us to life in your grace
and fill us with the hope of glory.
    Make us aware of all your gifts
that we may truly appreciate them
    We want to praise you not only with our lips
but in our lives, by serving you
    and by walking before you
in kindness and justice
    each day of our lives,
through Jesus Christ our Lord,
    to whom with you and the Holy Spirit,
be all honor and glory,
    world without end. Amen

                                    Autumn prayer

Thanksgiving

And turn to the Lord your God:
    for he is gracious and merciful,
slow to anger, and of great kindness.

Joel 2:13

Honor the Lord with substance,
    and with the firstfruits of all your increase.
So shall your barns be filled with plenty,
    and your presses shall burst out with new wine.

Proverbs 3:9-10

All the ends of the earth

Let the sea and what fills it resound,
    the world and those that dwell in it;
mountains shout with them
    for joy before the Lord,
for he comes, for he comes to rule the earth;
    he will rule the world with justice
and the people with equity.
    All the ends of the earth
have seen the salvation of our God.

Psalm 98:7-9

Love finds fulfillment

The whole person

Many a man, it is true, believes
    in the immortality of the soul;
but it is just the feeling of love above all
    which shows the inadequacy of this
abstract belief.
    A disembodied soul
is not a man, but an angel;
    but we love the man,
the whole human individuality,
    and if love is from the very first
the source of enlightenment
    and spiritualization
of this individuality,
    then it necessarily demands
the eternal youth and immortality
    of the determinate human being,
of this living soul incarnate
    in a bodily organism.

                                        Vladimir Solovyev

The fully grown person

There is a wholeness about the fully grown person
    which makes him concentrate on the present moment.
He may have unsatisfied desires,
    but he always keeps them out of sight,
and manages to master them some way or other.
    Clinging too much to our desires
easily prevents us from being what we ought to be
    and can be... We can have a full life
even when we haven't got everything we want.

The common denominator is to be sought
    both in thought and in practical living
in an integrated attitude to life.
    The person who allows himself to be torn
into fragments by events and problems
    has not passed the test
for the present and the future. ... We can never
    achieve this wholeness on our own;
it can only be acquired with the help of others.

Dietrich Bonhoeffer

A note on a lifetime

One of Napoleon's Old Guard presented to him, during an inspection, the following memo:

Joseph Durand:

Age 53
Years of service 26
Campaigns 14
Wounds 5
Children **8**
                                   ‾‾‾
T O T A L : 106

R E Q U E S T : "Legion of Honor"

Wisdom came to me

Wisdom is radiant and unfading,
and she is easily discerned by those
    who love her,
and is found by those who seek her.
She hastens to make herself known
    to those who desire her.
He who rises early to seek her
    will have no difficulty,
for he will find her sitting at his gates.
To fix one's thought on her
    is perfect understanding,
and he who is vigilant on her account
    will soon be free from care,
because she goes about seeking
    those worthy of her,
and she graciously appears to them
    in their paths,
and meets them in every thought.

The beginning of wisdom is the most sincere
    desire for instruction,
and concern for instruction
    is love of her,
and love of her is
    the keeping of her laws,
and giving heed to her laws
    is assurance of immortality,
and immortality brings one near to God;
so the desire for wisdom
    leads to a kingdom.

Wisdom of Solomon 6:12-20

Love finds a time for everything

For everything there is a season,
    and a time for every matter under heaven:
a time to be born, and a time to die;
    a time to plant, and a time to pluck up
        what is planted;
a time to kill, and a time to heal;
    a time to break down, and a time to build up;
a time to weep, and a time to laugh;
    a time to mourn, and a time to dance;
a time to cast away stones,
    and a time to gather stones together.

Ecclesiastes 3:1-5

Love penetrates the heart
of things

The personal mystery

In every soul ... there is an "abyss of mystery."
    Each person has his abyss
of which he is not aware,
    which he cannot know.
When hidden things shall have been revealed to us,
    according to the Promise,
there will be unimaginable surprises.
    The least of our actions resounds down
to infinite depths,
    and causes to shudder all the living
and all the dead,
    in such a way that each one
among the billions of human beings
    is truly *alone* before God.
Such is the abyss of our souls,
    such is their mystery.

                                        Leon Bloy

The center of life

The center of life is neither in thought
        nor in feeling, nor in will,
nor even in consciousness,
        so far as it thinks, feels, or wishes.
For moral truth may have been penetrated
        and possessed in all these ways,
and escape us still.
        Deeper even than consciousness
there is our being itself, our very substance,
        our nature. Only those truths
which have entered into this last region,
        which have become ourselves,
become spontaneous and involuntary,
        instinctive and unconscious,
are really our life-- that is to say,
        something more than our property.
So long as we are able to distinguish
        any space whatever
between the truth and us
        we remain outside it.

                                    Henri Frédéric Amiel

Touched by God

Late have I loved You,
    O beauty ever ancient, ever new!
Late have I loved You!
    And behold,
You were within, and I without,
    and without I sought You.
And deformed I ran after these forms
    of beauty You have made.
You were with me,
    and I was not with You,
those things held me back from You,
    things whose only being
was to be in You.
    You called; You cried;
and You broke through my deafness.
    You flashed; You shone;
and You chased away my blindness.
    You became fragrant;
and I inhaled and sighed for You.
    I tasted,
and now hunger and thirst
    for You.
You touched me:
    and I burned for Your embrace.

                                        Saint Augustine

                                                287

Knowing and longing

Knowledge seems more like a kind
    of pain-killing drug
that I have to take repeatedly
    against the boredom and desolation
of my heart.
    And no matter how faithful
I may be to it,
    it can never really cure me.
All it can give me is words and concepts,
    which perform the middleman's service
of expressing and interpreting reality
    to me, but can never still
my heart's craving for the reality itself,
    for true life and true possession.
I shall never be cured until all reality
    comes streaming like an ecstatic,
intoxicating melody into my heart.

Karl Rahner

Illumination

Having the eyes of your hearts
enlightened,
that you may know
what is the hope
to which he has called you.

Ephesians 1:18

A far deeper hope

There are two kinds of hope.
    First, the hope of success,
which gives men daring,
    and helps them win against odds.
That isn't the best sort of hope.
    It's dangerous like drug-taking.
You must keep on increasing the dose,
    and blind-folding your reason.
Men who do it are buoyant,
    self-confident,
but some of their integrity is lost.

The best kind of hope is not about success
    in this or that undertaking.
It's far deeper;
    hence when things go against you,
it isn't destroyed.
    It is hope about the nature
and future of man and the universe.

Clarence Day

Love is without illusion

To destroy illusions

I, of course, belong to a race
    which in the Middle Ages
was held responsible
    for all epidemics
and which today is blamed
    for the disintegration
of the Austrian Empire
    and the German defeat.
Such experiences have a sobering effect
    and are not conducive
to make one believe in illusions.
    A great part of my life's work
has been spent trying to destroy illusions
    of my own and those of mankind.
But if this one hope cannot be at least
    partially realized, if we don't learn
to divert our instincts
    from destroying our own kind,
what future lies in store for us?
    It is surely hard enough
to ensure the perpetuation of our species
    in the conflict between
our instinctual nature
    and the demands made upon us
by civilization.

Sigmund Freud

The price of life

For what does it profit a man,
    to gain the whole world
and forfeit his life?
    For what can a man give
in return for his life?

Mark 8:36-37

Personal happiness

Despite almost universal belief
    to the contrary,
gratification, ease, comfort, diversion
    and a state of having achieved
all one's goals
    do not constitute happiness for man.

We are coming to a conception of happiness
    that differs fundamentally
from the storybook version.
    The storybook conception
tells of desires fulfilled;
    the truer version involves
striving toward meaningful goals--
    goals that relate the individual
to a larger context of purposes.
    Storybook happiness
involves a bland idleness;
    the truer conception involves seeking
and purposeful effort.
    Storybook happiness involves every form
of pleasant thumb-twiddling;
    true happiness involves the full use
of one's powers and talents.
    Both conceptions of happiness
involve love,
    but the storybook version
puts great emphasis on being loved,
    the truer version more emphasis
on the capacity to give love.

                                    John W. Gardner

The world as it is

The Christian finds himself living a life
    which revolves in an eclipse about the two poles
of his faith and the world,
    poles in a relationship which can no longer be
clearly and obviously set and controlled by faith itself.
    He is aware that going along with the world
does not always result in going along with God.
    Such action often gets bogged down, as it were,
in the pure worldliness of the world.

Between the vision of faith and life
    as he finds it, therefore, the Christian
is aware of an ever-widening discrepancy.
    This difference cannot simply be disregarded
and left unresolved,
    for in the long run it will be taken up
and closed by the overpowering world of today
    and faith itself will become totally overshadowed
from the side of the world.
    Nor, if we take the wordliness of the world
with total Christian seriousness,
    can we resolve this difference
by making an act of faith in the God-centeredness
    of actual worldly events.
Rather, the believer ought to follow the pattern
    of Christ and "take up" the world,
even though it continue to seem unrelated to faith.

Johannes B. Metz

The measure of excellence

Nothing does more harm in unnerving men
    for their duties in the present than
the attention devoted to the points of
    excellence in the past as compared
with the average failure of the present day.

Alfred North Whitehead

The realistic imagination

Our use of the word imagination
     denotes two very different powers of mind.
One is the power to imagine things
     as they are not: this I call
the romantic imagination.
     The other is the power to imagine things
as they are without actually sensing them;
     and this I will call the realistic imagination.
Take for example marriage and war.
     One man has a vision of perpetual bliss
with a domestic angel at home,
     and of flashing sabres, thundering guns
and routed enemies in the field.
     That is a romantic imagination;
and the mischief it does is incalculable.
     It begins in silly and selfish expectations
of the impossible,
   and ends in spiteful disappointment.
The wise man knows that imagination
     is not only a means of pleasing himself
and beguiling tedious hours with romances and fairy tales...
     but also a means of foreseeing and being prepared
for realities as yet unexperienced,
     and of testing the possibility and desirability
of serious Utopias.

                                        George Bernard Shaw

The face of God

The spirit must constantly be on its guard
     against giving any particular image to the Godhead.
"In your longing to see the face of the Father in heaven,"
     says Evagrius, "never try to see any shape
or form when you are praying."
     "Do not wish to see angels or powers or Christ
with your senses or in the end you will become unbalanced,
taking the wolf for the shepherd, and worshipping evil spirits."

                                    Vladimir Lossky

A silent hope

Prayer ... though it accomplishes nothing material,
    constitutes something spiritual.
It will not bring rain, but until rain comes
    it may cultivate hope and resignation
and may prepare the heart for any issue,
    opening up a vista
in which human prosperity will appear
    in its conditioned existence
and conditional value.
    A candle wasting itself before an image
will prevent no misfortune,
    but it may bear witness to some silent hope
or relieve some sorrow by expressing it;
    it may soften a little the bitter sense
of impotence which would consume
    a mind aware of physical dependence
but not of spiritual dominion.

George Santayana

Love enjoys life

A wave of the hand

With all the powers of your body concentrated
    in the hand on the tiller,
All the powers of your mind concentrated
    on the goal beyond the horizon,
You laugh as the salt spray catches your face
    in the second of rest
Before a new wave--
Sharing the happy freedom of the moment
    with those who share your responsibility.
So-- in the self-forgetfulness of concentrated attention--
    the door opens for you into a pure living intimacy,
A shared, timeless happiness,
Conveyed by a smile,
A wave of the hand.

Thanks to those who have taught me this.
    Thanks to the days which have taught me this.

Dag Hammarskjold

All things new

Then I saw a new heaven and a new earth,
    for the first heaven and the first earth
had vanished, and there was no longer any sea.
    I saw the holy city, new Jerusalem,
coming down out of heaven from God,
    made ready like a bride adorned
for her husband.

I heard a loud voice proclaiming from the throne:
    "Now at last God has his dwelling
among men! He will dwell among them
    and they shall be his people,
and God himself will be with them.
    He will wipe every tear from their eyes;
there shall be an end to death,
    and to mourning and crying and pain;
for the old order has passed away!"

Revelation 21:1-5 (NEB)

If then our common life in Christ
     yields anything to stir the heart,
any loving consolation,
     any sharing of the Spirit,
any warmth of affection or compassion,
     fill up my cup of happiness
by thinking and feeling alike,
     with the same love for one another,
the same turn of mind,
     and a common care for unity.

Philippians 2:1-2 (NEB)

A marriage feast

There was a marriage at Cana in Galilee, and the mother of Jesus was there; Jesus also was invited to the marriage, with his disciples.

When the wine failed, the mother of Jesus said to him, "They have no wine."

And Jesus said to her, "O Woman, what have you to do with me? My hour has not yet come."

His mother said to the servants, "Do whatever he tells you."

Now six stone jars were standing there, for the Jewish rites of purification, each holding twenty or thirty gallons.

Jesus said to them, "Fill the jars with water," And they filled them up to the brim. He said to them, "Now draw some out, and take it to the steward of the feast." So they took it.

When the steward of the feast tasted the water now become wine, and did not know where it came from (though the servants who had drawn the water knew) the steward of the feast called the bridegroom and said to him, "Every man serves the good wine first; and when men have drunk freely, then the poor wine; but you have kept the good wine until now."

John 2:1-10

The ultimate perspective

The question whether human sin and suffering
    are finally evil and inimical to good
depends upon their eventual furtherance
    or prevention of the fulfillment of God's plan
for His creation.
    If man's pain and sin
are revealed in the final reckoning,
    at the end of human time,
as having frustrated God's purpose
    for His creatures,
then in that ultimate perspective
    they have been evil.
If, on the other hand, they have played
    a part in the fulfillment of that purpose,
then in the ultimate perspective
    they have contributed to good.

John Hick

Love faces old age and death

No one who waits for you
shall be put to shame.

Psalm 24:3

The value of man

I bid you put away anxious thoughts
    about food to keep you alive
and clothes to cover your body.
    Life is more than food,
the body more than clothes.
    Think of the ravens:
they neither sow nor reap;
    they have no storehouse or barn;
yet God feeds them.
    You are worth far more than the birds!
Is there a man among you
    who by anxious thought
can add a foot to his height?
    If, then, you cannot do
even a very little thing,
    why are you anxious about the rest?

Luke 12:22-26 (NEB)

The God who created the world and everything in it
    is himself the universal giver of life and breath
and all else. He created every race of men
    of one stock, to inhabit the whole earth's surface.
He fixed the epochs of their history
    and the limits of their territory.
They were to seek God and, it might be,
    touch and find him;
though indeed he is not far from each one of us,
    for in him we live and move, in him we exist.

Acts 17:25-27 (NEB)

Growing older

Can man live forever?
    Although no man may *wish* to live indefinitely,
it may be possible for death to be controlled
    so that all deaths
will be the result of accidents or suicide.
    What makes people grow old?
Gerontologists know that some
    very subtle changes take place
in an aging body.
    Cells die and are never replaced,
body water content drops,
    kidney plasma flow decreases.
Why? Perhaps the death of cells
    is a chance experience,
a result of an unfavorable mutation.
    Perhaps aging is the result
of a "time clock" within the cell
    which dictates its own demise.
A further understanding of molecular biology
    may provide insight into
and control of aging
    which will enable man
to select his own biological age.

Theodore J. Gordon

If there were no death in our world

Death is the most profound
    and significant fact of life:
it lifts the very last of mortals
    above the greyness
and banality of life.
    And only the fact of death
puts the question of life's meaning
    in all its depth.
Life in this world has meaning
    only because there is death:
if there were no death in our world,
    life would be deprived of meaning.
Meaning is linked with ending.
    And if there were no end,
if in our world there was evil
    and endlessness of life,
there would be no meaning to life whatever.
    The meaning of man's moral experience
throughout his whole life
    lies in putting him into a position
to comprehend death.

Nikolai Berdyaev

Accepting death

There is but one freedom,
     to put oneself right with death.
After that, everything is possible.
     I cannot force you
to believe in God.
     Believing in God amounts to
coming to terms with death.
     When you have accepted death,
the problem of God will be solved--
     and not the reverse.

Albert Camus

My faith in You is nothing but
     the dark path in the night
between the abandoned shack
     of my poor, dim earthly life
and the brilliance of your Eternity.

Karl Rahner

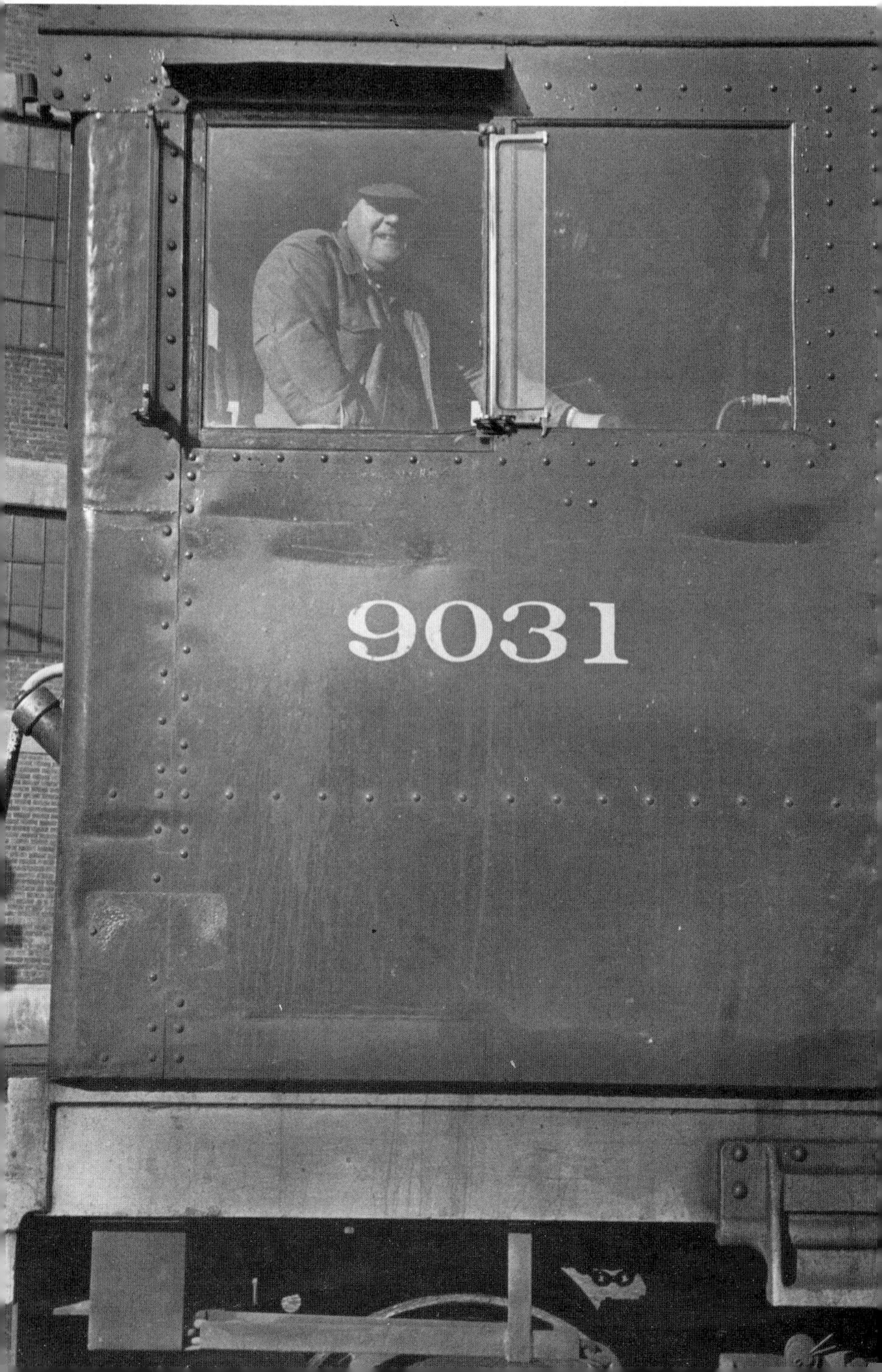
9031

Where your wealth is

Provide for yourselves purses
      that do not wear out,
and never-failing wealth in heaven,
      where no thief can get near it,
no moth destroy it.
      For where your wealth is
there will your heart be also.

Luke 12:33-34 (NEB)

There are many who say, "O that we
      might see some good!
Lift up the light of thy countenance
      upon us, O Lord!"
Thou has put more joy in my heart
      than they have when their grain
and wine abound.
      In peace I will both lie down and sleep;
for thou alone, O Lord, makes me
      dwell in safety.

Psalm 4:6-8

Love contains giant possibilities

It is our decision

We have the power to make this the best generation
  in the history of mankind, or to make it the last.

I believe we have made our decision
  and made it known to the world.

                              John F. Kennedy

The power of faith

Faith is not simply an intellectual assent
        to Christian dogma. Taken in a much richer sense,
faith involves a belief in God that arouses us
        to action, that fills us with a lived conviction
that the universe is permeated with a redeeming love.
        God did not create men and women
as automated robots or helpless puppets,
        but enabled them somehow to shape
their own destiny within the innumerable possibilities
        created by his divine love. Such a faith
gives meaning to human love--and to life itself.

                                        Thomas J. O'Connor

You have not seen him, yet you love him;
    and trusting in him now without seeing him,
you are transported with a joy too great for words,
    while you reap the harvest of your faith,
that is, salvation for your souls. This salvation
    was the theme which the prophets pondered
and explored, those who prophesied about the grace
    of God awaiting you. They tried to find out
what was the time, and what the circumstances,
    to which the spirit of Christ in them pointed,
foretelling the sufferings in store for Christ
    and the splendors to follow.

1 Peter 1:8-12

If we do not believe, the waves engulf us,
    the winds blow, nourishment fails,
sickness lays us low or kills us,
    the divine power is impotent or remote.
If, on the other hand, we believe,
    the waters are welcoming and sweet,
the bread is multiplied, our eyes open,
    the dead rise again,
the power of God is, as it were
    drawn from him by force
and spreads throughout all nature.

Teilhard de Chardin

323

There is a future for the man of peace.

Psalm 36:37

Fashioning mankind

If, to take a more personal case,
    I decide to marry and to have children,
even though this decision proceeds simply
    from my situation, from my passion
or desire, I am thereby committing not only
    myself, but humanity as a whole,
to the practice of monogamy. I am thus
    responsible for myself and for all men,
and I am creating a certain image for
    myself and for all men, and I am
creating a certain image of man as I
    would have him to be. In fashioning
myself I fashion man.
    When a man commits himself to anything,
fully realizing that he is not only choosing
    what he will be, but is thereby
at the same time a legislator deciding
    for the whole of mankind--in such a moment
a man cannot escape from the sense of
    complete and profound responsibility.

                                Jean-Paul Sartre

A moment of peace

Around us in a half circle
      the front quickened to a distant,
incoherent fusillade that rolled across
      the sky like pebbles
flung up and sucked back by the tide.
      At times the firing spread out
twenty miles and more along the line
      like an epidemic, like the flames
from firedamp. Then everything subsided,
      fell quiet, and withdrew into itself.
It is in such moments of unbroken silence
      that you hear war dying.
All hatreds are relinquished,
      and one instant of such calm is
enough to change the face of the world.
      There is no need to return a blow,
no need to await a counterblow,
      no need to snatch up any challenge.
This is the chance never to fire another shot,
      and the heart stops beating.

                                    Antoine de Saint-Exupery

And the land had rest from war.

Joshua 11:23

The Spirit will speak

And be on your guard,
    for men will turn you over to their courts,
they will flog you, and you will be brought
    before governors and kings,
for my sake, to testify before them.

But when you are arrested,
    do not worry about what you are to say;
when the time comes,
    the words you need will be given you;
for it is not you who will be speaking:
    it will be the Spirit of your Father
speaking in you.

So do not be afraid of them.
    There is nothing covered up
that will not be uncovered, nothing hidden
    that will not be made known.
What I say to you in the dark
    you must repeat in broad daylight;
what you hear whispered
    you must shout from the housetops.

Matthew 10:17-20; 26-27 (NEB)

Do you know that in a race
     all the runners compete,
but only one receives the prize?
     So run that you may obtain it.

1 Corinthians 9:24

Love sees no end

You will eat what your hands have worked for,
happiness and prosperity will be yours.

Psalm 128:2 (JB)

Confidence in the future

The West has marked itself off from other cultures
        precisely by its confidence in the future.
The religious form of this confidence is most identified
 with Saint Augustine, who, breaking with the cyclic theories
 in which time was a great wheel turning around itself,
 asserted the pilgrimage of history toward the City of God.
The secular version of the same hope dates at least
        from the Renaissance and culminates in the capitalist
and socialist vision of progress.

Along with this futurism there was the affirmation
        of the power of reason.
Without rational human direction, the accidental revolution
        is not moving toward rebirth
but toward an inhuman collectivism.

                                        Michael Harrington

Our unfinished world

I think the true discovery
    of America is before us.
I think the true fulfillment
    of our spirit, of our people,
of our mighty and immortal land,
    is yet to come...
certain as the morning,
    inevitable as noon.

Thomas Wolfe

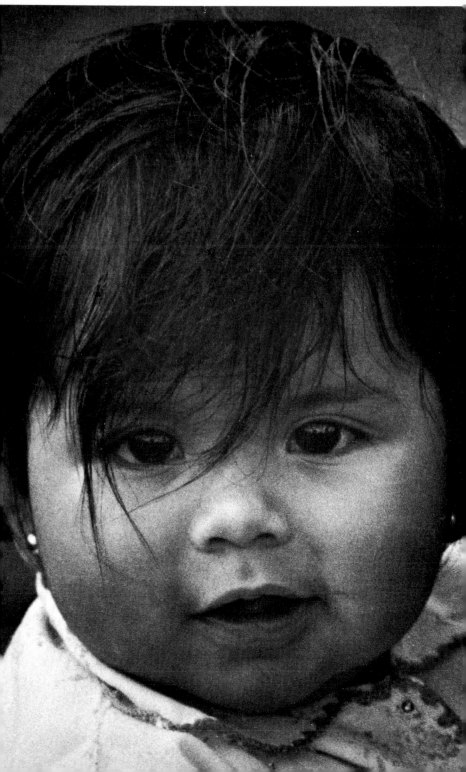

We are to grow up in every way
    into him who is the head,
into Christ, from whom the whole body,
    joined and knit together
by every joint with which it is supplied,
    when each part is working properly,
makes bodily growth and upbuilds itself
    in love.

Ephesians 4:15-16

Mankind linked together

All nations are selfish.
    All nations consider
their selfishness sacred.
    It may be
that your consciousness
    of your material power
will one day cause you
    to take advantages.
Look, my American friends,
    it seems to me
that something new is in formation
    on our planet.
The material progress of modern times
    has indeed linked mankind
by a sort of nervous system.
    The contacts are innumerable.
The communications are instantaneous.
    We are materially bound
like the cells of the same body.
    But this body
does not yet have a soul.
    This organism has not yet
grown conscious of itself.
    The hand does not feel itself
a part with the eye.

Antoine de Saint-Exupery

Without killing

If we can actually set up a social structure
    that will enable us to live together
without killing ourselves,
    it will ... give us the time we need
to understand and develop
    our full biological potentialities ...
Our eyes and ears
    that give out when we are old,
our hearts and arteries,
    why not make them better biologically?
We begin to see the possibility
    of reshaping the human organism,
as we have been reshaping
    plant and animal organisms now
for many years.
    Man will cease to be at the mercy
of the evolutionary accidents
    that made his frame and his society.
It will be a time
    when man can begin
to plan what he wants to be.

John Rader Platt

We have stood the test

Therefore, now that we have been justified
    through faith, let us continue at peace
with God through our Lord Jesus Christ,
    through whom we have been allowed to enter
the sphere of God's grace,
    where we now stand. Let us exult
in the hope of the divine splendor
    that is to be ours. More than this:
let us even exult in our present sufferings,
    because we know that suffering trains us
to endure, and endurance brings proof
    that we have stood the test,
and this proof is the ground of hope.
    Such a hope is no mockery,
because God's love has flooded
    our inmost heart
through the Holy Spirit he has given us.

Romans 5:1-5 (NEB)

Hope for mankind

Paul's hope for the Christian community
     expresses the Christian hope for man--
for the past, the present,
     and (in a special way) the future
of mankind.
     It is the hope that he
who raised up Jesus Christ
     will raise man up also.
It is the hope
     that he will bring the race of men,
as well as the individual person
     and the community of Christians,
to the measure of the stature
     of the maturity of Christ.
In this hope,
     the future of man
is seen as a dynamic evolutionary movement
     toward increasingly greater
and more perfect maturity
     in the context of his transformed
and deified humanity.
     To put it another way,
Christians today have no message
     more central or more important
to give to mankind:
     He lives, and you will live.

Thomas P. Collins

339

Two stages of creation

This was indeed God's pleasure--
 to divide the whole creation
into two stages:
 the present one
in which he made everything changeable
 and the one which will be,
when by renewing everything
 he will make it changeless.
The foundation of these things
 God shows us in the...Lord Christ,
who took his existence from us
 and was raised by the Father
from the dead
 and made changeless
in body and soul.
 Here he showed
that this would happen
 to the entire creation.

Theodore of Mopsuestia

The future good

For I am sure that neither death, nor life,
    nor angels, nor principalities, nor things present,
nor things to come, nor powers, nor height,
    nor depth, nor any other creature
will be able to separate us from the love of God,
    which is in Christ Jesus our Lord.

Romans 8:38-39

We do not know in what ways or in what scale of time
    God is bringing future good out of present evil;
but that He *is* doing so, and that we can therefore
    commit ourselves wholly to His providence,
is the practical outcome of faith in God's love
    and sovereignty seen in the life, death
and resurrection of the Christ.

John Hick

A sense of eternity

Our sense of immortality
    lies in conscience.
It lies decisively in love,
    that wondrous reality--
we are mortal when we are loveless,
    immortal when we love.
Our love for the dead
    would be faithless
if it lost its sense of eternity.
    Immortality does not happen
by itself.
    One whose life is fulfilled
in the present--"immortal"--
    bears the future in time.
One whose present life is empty
    bears no future.

Karl Jaspers

Adventures into life

Perhaps there *are* challenges and tasks,
    problems and pains in heaven.
For the Christian conception of heaven
    is not basically that of a pain-free paradise,
but that of life lived
    in a wholly right relationship to God.
There may be endless scope for further
    discovery and exploration,
further adventures
    in new dimensions of reality,
further experiments
    in new sciences
and experiences in new arts,
    further spiritual growth
in relation to the infinite
    divine plenitude and activity.
But our imaginative resources
    are so utterly inadequate
to whatever the power and wisdom
    of God may have in store for
"just men made perfect"
    that these are probably
all but childish guesses.

                                        John Hick

All times are his seasons

God made sun and moon to distinguish seasons,
    and day and night,
and we cannot have the fruits of the earth
    but in their seasons;
but God hath made no decree to distinguish the seasons
      of his mercies;
    in paradise the fruits were ripe the first minute,
and in heaven it is always autumn,
    his mercies are ever at their maturity.
God never says, you should have come yesterday;
    he never says, you must come again tomorrow,
but today if you will hear his voice,
    today he will hear you.
He brought light out of darkness,
    not out of lesser light;
he can bring thy summer out of winter,
    though thou have no spring.
All occasions invite his mercies,
    and all times are his seasons.

John Donne

ACKNOWLEDGMENTS

Abingdon Press for the poem "Discovery" from *Songs from the Slums* by Toyohiko Kagawa. Copyright renewal 1963 by Lois J. Erickson. Used by permission of Abingdon Press.

Argus Communications for excerpts from *Christian Involvement,* by Bernard Cooke. Copyright © 1966 by Argus Communications.

Harcourt, Brace & World, Inc. for the poem "To Look at Any Thing" from *The Living Seed,* copyright © 1961 by John Moffitt. Reprinted by permission of Harcourt, Brace & World, Inc.

Harper & Row for an excerpt from *The Divine Milieu* by Pierre Teilhard de Chardin. Copyright © 1957 by Editions de Seuil, Paris. English translation copyright © 1960 by William Collins Sons & Co., Ltd., London, and Harper & Row, Publishers, Incorporated, New York. Also for an excerpt from *Hymn of the Universe,* by Pierre Teilhard de Chardin. Copyright © 1965 in the English translation by William Collins Sons & Co., Ltd., London, and Harper & Row, Publishers, Incorporated, New York. Also for an excerpt from *Evil and the God of Love,* by John Hick. Copyright © 1966 by John Hick. Used by permission of Harper & Row, Publishers.

Carl Wendell Hines, Jr., for permission to reprint lines from "Two Jazz Poems," copyright © 1963 by the author.

Alfred A. Knopf, Inc., for the poem "Dreams" from *The Dreamkeeper,* by Langston Hughes. Copyright 1932, by Alfred A. Knopf, Inc., renewed 1960 by Langston Hughes, and used by permission of the publisher.

PHOTO CREDITS

American Machine and Foundry Company 138, 146

Laurence B. Fink 26, 36, 39, 40, 52, 63, 71, 72, 98, 105, 106, 112, 118, 135, 136, 154, 162, 169, 173, 177, 183, 189, 193, 195, 199, 207, 209, 210, 215, 216, 235, 236, 242, 247, 250, 258, 283, 289, 299, 302, 307, 312, 317, 318

Jerry Frank 22, 44, 47, 67, 149. 190, 202, 218, 263, 333

General Dynamics Corporation 152

Ralph D. McKinney 10, 15, 68, 267, 346

Fortune Monte 12, 16, 19, 20, 29, 64, 79, 92, 100, 103, 133, 141, 142, 145, 181, 185, 201, 213, 223, 230, 240, 245, 279, 284, 295, 308, 311, 324, 334, 342

NASA 115, 224

Sylvia Plachy 8, 24, 36, 58, 60, 74-75, 88, 101, 108, 120, 123, 161, 167, 275, 290

Norman Provost, FSC 35, 86, 130, 158, 186, 253, 254, 337

Edward Rice 33, 48, 50, 126, 128, 164, 273

Standard Oil Company 229

United Nations 56, 82, 268, 292, 304, 329, 330, 341

United States Army 76

United States Rubber Company 91, 157, 320